To my Mom, Dad, Haden, and Austin

Lauren,

Enjoy!

Things in my Pocket

Contents

Things in my Pocket

Preface

On April 23rd, 2022 I received a call from Riley, a concerned sister to a close friend of mine letting me know that my friend who was staying at my house that weekend had just been in a severe cycling accident. Drew, a five foot seven, 2021 grad from Hope College and financial analyst at J.P Morgan with dark brown hair combed over and glasses, has a passion for cycling that he can not contain, even on a weekend trip to visit me. Drew had left that morning around nine am to go on a two-three hour bike ride, training for a race he was planning to compete in. That morning I was volunteering as a business major panelist for new students at Hope College to meet the department. At around noon, I was shopping in the Hope College bookstore when I got a call from his sister, who told me that Drew was in the hospital and that she was leaving Grand Rapids to be with him. I immediately left, and spent the next four hours sitting in the ER with him as he got x-rays, CT scans and stitches to his left eyebrow, outer upper lip and inside his lower lip. Fortunately, he did not have any serious breaks or injuries, and was left with only stitches and a concussion.

Things in my Pocket

After Drew was discharged from the hospital, I asked Riley and Drew how I was contacted because I knew Riley did not have my phone number. Drew explained how when the EMTs got to the scene, they found him unconscious in a ditch. He didn't know how he got there; whether he was hit, run off the road, or simply fell off his bike. Either way, one of the local residents that lived in that area found Drew lying there and called an ambulance. The EMTs did their job and lifted Drew into the ambulance, where he gave them the password to his phone. They called his most recent contact. This contact was Drew's now girlfriend, who answered the phone comically with, "What's up, bitch?" The EMT responded with all seriousness, "This is Mike, your friend Drew was just in a cycling accident and is on his way to the Holland Hospital. Do you understand?" As well intended the joke was, Drew's girlfriend quickly ate her words.

The EMT also called Drew's dad who was much more helpful at the time. His dad called Riley who then called me. It all made sense, but it left me in deep reflection. If Drew would not have had his phone on him, how would any of us have found out what happened? If he hadn't put his wallet in his pocket, along with his phone, how would the EMTs have identified him? The most important question I was left thinking about was, if I was found unconscious in a ditch what would someone find in my pockets? After I thought about it, there are ten things someone can find in my pockets on any given day:

1. A phone
2. A wallet
3. A set of car keys
4. A notebook
5. A pair of sunglasses
6. A set of airpods
7. A pen
8. A cross
9. A pocket knife
10. A coin

The story of Drew is relevant to this book because it was the inspiration for the title and the overall cohesion of seemingly independent stories. For the last three years, I have spent my free time writing stories of my childhood, of my friends, and of my family. However, it lacked a spine, a theme to weave through its entirety. Things in my Pocket is an illustration that without our stories, without our memories, we are merely unconscious bodies in a ditch.

Like you, I have lived through perpetuated elections, a global pandemic, and experienced trauma that has made me the person I am today. You may be asking, "why should I read this book?" and my answer is based on the acknowledgement of my privilege, my ignorance, and my lack of life experience in general as a way to establish my credibility. I am a 21-year-old white male from the Midwest of the United States. My father works in construction and my mother is a school teacher. I write this book to share my familial history through influential stories in my life. Each story, each memory, has made me who I am today. I write for personal reflection, meditation and healing and I invite you to do the same as you read this book. My hope is that it creates space for you. You may not walk away enlightened or changed, but I hope as you read about my life to this point and compare it to your own experience, you are able to reflect on the transitions in your own life. At the very least, you will walk away entertained by stories I have to share. And just maybe you will learn a lesson, start a new habit, or come away with a new perspective and a greater appreciation for life. That is my goal, my hope, and my prayer for you as you read this book.

One

Phone

In 2001, I was introduced to this world and I believe I am part of the last generation to live before the overwhelming incorporation of technology. I am part of the last generation of children to start their telecommunication lives with a flip phone. When I was 14 years old, my parents bought me a classic flip phone that I could take to middle school with me. This flip phone was capable of calling my mom to pick me up after school and send very simple texts. In middle school, I would walk outside after class and call my mom to let her know I was ready to be picked up. Then I would entertain myself by talking to my classmates, staring at the sky, or swinging around a parking lot sign post. The phone in my pocket was for security and communication purposes only. A part of me misses those simpler days, and if you ask anyone they will tell you I am still a very simple texter.

As time has gone on and I have transitioned through life, so too has the type of phone I carry in my pocket. It was about my freshman year, in 2015, when I was handed my first iPhone. From then on, Google, YouTube, and iTunes made life that much more convenient. I was fortunate enough to be on the concluding end of the Vine era, and I'm sure if you search hard enough you will find some old, cringey vines of a very young, chubby Ethan Getchell with slicked over hair lip-singing into his camera to taco cat lyrics.

Social media has intrigued me and baffled me since its introduction. From Vine to YouTube to Instagram to TikTok, I was attracted to creating content and entertaining anyone who would take the time to watch. After my middle school to high school "vine" days, I continued to post on Instagram, Twitter, Snapchat, and Facebook like every other kid did at the time. But in 2018, I had an idea.

My brother Haden and I have always had a connection and hilarious banter between each other. We could be in school, in church, or in a random Arby's and end up making everyone (mostly ourselves) roll on the floor, crying in laughter. We recognized this banter and wanted to document it, share it, and honestly gain as much attention as we could. So on Christmas in 2018, we asked our parents for a Canon camera, camera mount, studio light and backdrop; We were going to start a YouTube channel. We came up with a plan to do a 4 part series focused on brothers pranking each other, getting revenge and honestly taking turns making each other look like fools. We advertised and hyped up our premiere video, and at the start of 2019 we published our first YouTube video.

The video was ridiculously long, poorly edited and very obviously our first stab at being "youtubers". However, our first video amassed over 10,000 views as people watched Haden give me a haircut and bleach my hair. We brainstormed how to get even more views and keep up the hype, so we decided that piercing Haden's belly button was the obvious option. With no prior experience and little to no rational guidance (or reception of given guidance), I successfully pierced Haden's belly button for the whole world to see. Viewers were shocked, people couldn't believe what we were doing, but they couldn't stop watching. As far as our small town of Portland, Michigan with a population of 5,000 goes, we were a hit.

We dialed it back, did more trendy videos like the bird box challenge, yoga challenge and did classic YouTube influencer videos. But we also did unique videos like interviewing our exchange student and all the exchange students at our high school. The peak of our YouTube fame was when we created a GoFundMe to support the IMKids Third Meal Food Pantry in their peanut butter drive. Haden and I were both part of the Youth Advisory Council in our county, a collection of high school representatives from every school in the county who worked for the betterment of our community. Haden and I used our Youtube platform to raise over $500 - which is a lot for two kids in high school. We posted a video announcing our need, with the goal to make a follow up video of our progress. The best part was filming ourselves going to CostCo and buying $500 worth of peanut butter, stuffing it in the trunk of a two seater Audi TT, and carrying it into the food pantry. The reactions were priceless and the videos of us swimming in the jars of peanut butter in our basement are hilarious to watch. The local Ionia County News even asked to interview us and let us shout out our YouTube channel.

Over time, it became difficult to continue making YouTube videos. I had to work that summer, Haden had summer workouts for football, and I had to prepare to move to college. When I moved to Hope in the fall, I tried to continue making YouTube videos with my new roommate, Josh Haddad. One weekend we went to see Kanye West's Sunday Service in Detroit on a Friday, followed by a Chance the Rapper concert in Chicago that Saturday. In between we stopped at an iHop in Detroit where we ran into Kim Kardashian and her family. The content was great but it wasn't the same as doing it with my brother.

Spring 2020 rolled around, and with it all that was the COVID-19 pandemic. I was on spring break in Tennessee when I learned that Hope College was going into quarantine and we would not be returning to campus. As I drove home, my mom and two brothers, Haden and Austin, were just leaving to go on their high school spring break to Florida. They rented an AirBnB in West Palm Beach and kept to themselves for the most part, so the reality of the pandemic had not set in. Since I didn't have to go back to school, they invited me to drive down and be with them. I called my friend Emie Ross and asked if she wanted to ride along with me. She agreed and we left that night, driving 20 hours from Michigan to Florida straight through.

About that same time, TikTok was at the peak of its existence. People were starting to quarantine so people had nothing else to do but dance in their rooms and watch other people do just that. As a retired YouTuber, loyal to the brand, I refused to join TikTok… at first. It wasn't until my mom's request that I agreed to make a TikTok with her.

We were on a run in sunny Florida when my mom was starting to lose momentum. As a way to raise her spirit, I told her I was making a TikTok, raising my camera into the air in selfie mode to record the two of us. I asked her how she was feeling and she said something along the lines of, "We're 3 miles in and I'm about to pee myself. Go Mama!" A 15 second video that I recorded and discarded in my camera roll.

A few days later my mom asked for an update on our TikTok and I told her I didn't actually post it. She was devastated and I felt guilty, so I posted the video. The first day nothing happened, but the second day was much different. We all sat there as the video climbed 100 views, 1000 views, 10,000 views, 100,000 views, until it peaked at over 400,000 views. Haden and I thought people loved us, but TikTok loved my mom.

The rest of that vacation and the majority of the pandemic consisted of "Go Mama" content, recording videos with my mom singing, dancing, sleeping, cooking and doing everything she does on a normal day. It was never the elaborate, well planned TikToks that did well, rather the random 15 second sweaty runs together with a simple quip followed by "Go Mama!" Together we gained over 50,000 followers on TikTok and we have never had so much fun as a family, spending time together in quarantine, recording our lives, documenting memories and sharing them with the world.

I wish I could say that the story ends here, but I feel obligated to share the ugly along with the glamor. In a perfect world, this fame and popularity (as small as it was in reality) would only do good and benefit me and the people who enjoy watching my family. However, I let the influence I had get to my head. I was single at this time and I had attractive girls adding me on all forms of social media. The negative side effects of a phone and social media is that it dehumanizes people to a point where you don't even think you are talking to an actual person on the other end. You post, get views and sometimes even make money. You start to think you can say and post whatever you want. Until you take it too far.

By this time, the era of TikTok was dwindling, at least for my family and me. I was back at school and I had responsibilities to prioritize. Even though I wasn't making TikToks, I still had connections to random people all over the world. Random connections on Snapchat, mixed with the separation from identity that social media and technology encourage, created a toxic environment where I began sending just about anything to anyone. The short term satisfaction for approval from strangers does not outway the long term lack of respect I was creating for myself. And I wish I was able to stop before it hurt myself, and other people.

In the spring of 2022, I received a DM from a random account on Instagram that said they had explicit images of me and they were going to share them with the world if I did not cooperate. I knew better than to listen to them, so I deleted the message. The account continued to contact me, until I made it clear I would not cooperate. At that point, they created a fake account of me and posted all the explicit images they had of me. This fake account requested to follow me and my heart sank. They continued to blackmail me and told me if I did not cooperate they would follow all my friends and family. I chose not to cooperate and blocked the account. The account then proceeded to follow all of my friends and family. My world came crashing in.

I called my parents, hoping to get to them before they saw. I can't put into words how grateful I am for the unconditional love and support they showed me. As time went on, family members, college friends, hometown friends, teachers, professors and what felt like every single person in the whole world were seeing these images. My biggest fear the entire time was that people would judge me, look at me differently and not want anything to do with me. In reality, not one person was anything but loving and understanding through it all. When people reached out, they were asking how I was doing, how they could support me, and what they could do to make this go away.

The most concerning and enlightening part of the whole experience was when the account went live and I called the police. I talked to local law enforcement, the FBI and even the Hope College Campus Safety. They all said the same thing - there was nothing they could do. A friend of ours in law enforcement shared with my family and I that the worst part of this all is that it happens all the time. The difference is these accounts go after 14 year old girls and persuade them to send explicit images, then blackmail their families with them. The impact can be devastating. I found out that a young man my same age committed suicide because this same thing happened to him.

I know exactly what it feels like to have your whole world cave in. To feel hopeless. To not have any answers or solutions to the problem. My junior year of college was the first time I had an overwhelming panic attack. It was also the first time I went to therapy. My peace, my reassurance and my life had to be put back together. The glue and healing I owe to my friends, my family and my faith in God.

So when I look at my phone now, it is not with the same excitement that 15 year old Ethan looked at his first iPhone with, but rather an anxious feeling that at any moment I could receive a DM or message that flips my world upside down. I no longer idolize social media and prioritize it in my life. If you search for me now you will not find me on Snapchat, Instagram, Twitter or YouTube. Even though these platforms are stained with the decisions I chose to make, the memories I made with my friends and family remain pure in my heart.

I continue to walk through life with a phone in my pocket. I have flipped the page, continuing to transition and grow in life. From a flip phone, to a smartphone, to social media fame, to reality today, technology has left a mark on who I am as a person. Pictures and videos in my phone serve as artifacts of memories both good and bad. If someone were to find my phone and get in, they would know who I am as a person, for better or for worse. Regardless, they have made me who I am today.

Two

Wallet

Besides having a phone, the other most common item I keep in my pocket is my wallet. It's funny to think about the evolution of a wallet as you get older. I started out with one of my dad's hand me down wallets, collecting more slushie cards than dollars. Over time credit cards, business cards, dollar bills and IDs stretched the wallet until it barely fit in my pocket. There are two types of people in this world; those with fat wallets that look like mini Bibles, and those with skinny wallets that are trying to be trendy. I have been the owner of both.

When I think about my dad's hand me down wallet, I think about the financial advice he has given me. My dad is a very financially responsible person. When he was first married to my mom, they moved to Portland, Michigan to plant roots and start a family. In order to pay off my mom's college debt, they would buy houses, live in them while they renovated them, and flip them for profit. This method established a sense of appreciation for investing in long term welfare. Even though the work was hard and the moves were difficult, the desire for financial independence was stronger.

Things in my Pocket

At a young age, my parents encouraged my brothers and me to be entrepreneurial. Between my brothers and me, we saved up our money and bought a goldendoodle. We named her Minnie. Once she was old enough, we bred her and sold her puppies to our community. My mom helped us, and honestly did most of the grunt work, marketing on Facebook and cleaning up after the puppies. My brothers and I helped her do this three times with three litters. The first litter was my responsibility, the second was Haden's and the third was Austin's. The profits from each litter were used to help my brothers and I buy our first vehicles when we were old enough. When I was 16, I bought a 2001 silver Ford F-150 for five thousand dollars. I drove this truck for the entirety of my high school career. It transported me to wrestling practices, late night Taco Bell runs and my girlfriend's house on the weekends. I remember doing donuts in the high school back parking lot during the winter, and setting up the tent made for the bed of my truck in the summer. The money in my wallet is representative of the transitions in life as my parents helped me become financially and personally independent.

From my admiration for my parents and their continued mentorship, I thought about how I could live into this myself. My Aunt Kayla once shared how she picked up a new side hustle where she goes on Facebook Marketplace, finds free furniture, and picks it up. She then cleans the furniture, takes high quality photos of them, and sells them on Facebook Marketplace for anywhere from one hundred to one thousand dollars. After hearing about my aunt's success, I thought out how I could make this a reality for myself. The problem was I didn't have a truck, trailer or anywhere to store the couches. Fortunately, I knew someone with all of these things.

Parker Bos is a close friend of mine, brother in the Arcadian Fraternity and college housemate. Parker is from Holland, Michigan and his family built large machinery warehouses behind their house. He has a snowmobile trailer that is enclosed and a truck that was a gift from his grandfather. I told Parker about the crazy idea and he loved it.

We did a test run one Saturday. I went on Facebook Marketplace, found about ten couches within a thirty mile radius, and we spent the entire day driving around picking up free furniture. Some of the furniture was better than others. One couch was not worth keeping, but we took the couch because the owners were an older couple that wanted to get rid of it and we knew they would not get it out on their own. We found that we were providing a service as much as we were providing a product. We never lied when people asked what we planned to do with the furniture, and most people admired our entrepreneurial spirits.

Parker and I brought the couches back to his house, cleaned and sanitized them, put them up on Facebook Marketplace, and priced them with help from my aunt. We had about five thousand dollars in inventory and made about four thousand dollars profit after expenses from that first Saturday. We became excited, realizing that this could be a sustainable project for the rest of our college careers.

With savings, investments, and long term welfare in mind, we decided to meet with multiple mentors to help guide our next steps. We met with a real estate agent, Steve Grilley, who told us we should start an LLC to centralize our money and put terms of agreement on paper. From there, we met with Bill Sikkel, a lawyer in Holland, who helped us write up our operation agreement.

Lastly, we met with Parker's accountant who helped us get our finances in order so that everything we did was legal and on record for taxes. Just like that, we had an LLC with a federal tax ID to open a savings account for our couch profits. We named our business *KJ Real Estate LLC* in honor of our grandfathers who had passed away, Ken Assink and John Getchell.

We continue to have a lot of fun with our couch business. On Facebook Marketplace, our commerce page is titled Bos and Getchell's Flipping Fast Furniture. We even made business cards. One creative marketing tactic I came up with was to post the couches on the Hope College Garage Sale site on Facebook. We have never sold a couch from that site, but what it did was get our name out there. People started asking Parker and me what we were doing, and this opened up leads to people who either wanted us to take their couches or were interested in buying one.

People have asked us about the ethics behind our business. I think it is rather straightforward. People don't have the time or energy to sell their furniture so we do them a service by picking it up for them. Then we clean the furniture and sell it for money, emphasizing free delivery. So many stores are backed up due to factors such as the global pandemic, so by offering free delivery people are more willing to buy our furniture.

Parker and I have learned a lot through this journey. My brother Haden has even started doing this back home with intentions of joining our business when he gets to Hope. We have made a lot of connections, served a lot of people and learned a lot about what it takes to run a business. Our goal is to work hard this summer, save our money and use it to get into real estate in the Holland area.

This spontaneous entrepreneurship is not singular to the couch business. My brother and I also sold sweatshirts in our free time. Our uncles inspired us, as they started their own framing business years ago, Getchell Brothers Framing. They created sweatshirts for their business that have become Haden's and my favorite sweatshirts to wear. As they succeeded and grew, they evolved from Getchell Brothers Framing to GBI DRW. With this new identity and brand, they had no use for their old one, so they gave it to Haden and me. We erased the framing part of the logo and created sweatshirts that just have Getchell Brothers on them. We have had friends and family come up and ask us if they could buy our sweatshirts from us, so instead of giving them ours, we made more. Getchell Brother sweatshirts are available for purchase and embody the values of family, brotherhood, hardwork and love.

When I wear my Getchell Brothers sweatshirt, I think about my dad and my uncles. I think about their strong familial bonds. I think about their love for each other and for the work that they do. I think about the Getchell name and my desire to honor and uplift the name. When I see people wearing our sweatshirts around campus, I am honored and emotional at the fact that brotherhood, family, is not confined to nuclear ties. My family has taught me to welcome others in and treat them as family. When you wear a Getchell Brothers sweatshirt, I hope you feel the same sense of pride and responsibility. When you see a Getchell Brothers logo, I hope you see my brother's faces, their smiles and their warm welcomes.

When I give someone a sweatshirt, a couch or a business card, I think about why I do what I do. I have been called sporadic, crazy, energized. I seem to have a new project every two weeks. From YouTube and TikTok, to couches and sweatshirts, my passion and motivation is to invest in my future and those around me. I am driven by significance, competition, focus and lifelong learning. It is the driving factor behind this book.

Valuing significance means that I pour my energy into what will make the most impact on me, my friends and my community. Competition helps me reflect on what I do well and what I lack, using that to help me and help others. Focus allows me to harness this energy and craziness for good. Lifelong learning surrounds all these things. I believe the moment you stop learning in what you do is the moment you lose sight of the significance, which destroys any focus. I am reminded of these values when I feel the wallet in my pocket. The money, the cards, the IDs are all reminders of precious memories that have shaped me and helped me transition over time.

Three

Car Keys

Tucked between my phone and wallet, you will find a set of keys. These keys have changed over time. Car keys may be one of the biggest influences on my transitions in life, transporting me from one season to the next. I currently own a 2005 white Infiniti M35. As you know, before the Infiniti I drove a truck. Sadly, when it came time to transition to college, it was economically beneficial for me to get a new vehicle. I gave my beloved truck to my brother Haden, who turned around and sold my truck as soon as I left. On the bright side, my mom was driving the Infiniti at the time and she gave it to me as a going away present. This Infiniti is also sentimental because of its tie to my family. Before my mom owned this Infiniti, it belonged to Alene Harris. Tom and Alene Harris have a unique relationship to my family and are two of the most important people in my life.

My mom, Theresa Dawn Medley, was born and raised in the heart of the South. I could write a whole book on the upbringing of my mom, but to make a long story short, it looked exactly like it sounds when I say "born and raised in the Appalachian Mountains." Wagons, welfare, and weed - the definition of "yeehaw". My mom was the oldest child, with one younger sister, Cricket. Theresa and Cricket raised hell growing up; drawing on walls, getting in fights, crashing mopeds and busting their heads open crashing those mopeds. My mom's first driving experience was a P.O.S that had a driver side door that was a different color from the rest and a passenger side that was missing a floorboard. You had to keep your knees in your chest when you rode with Theresa so you didn't get road burns.

My mom grew up with divorced parents, bouncing around from place to place, determined to make a life for herself, fueled by her love for learning. She was different from the folks she grew up with. She was bright and she was motivated. When my mom was little she would sit Cricket down in a chair and use the wall at home as a chalkboard as she taught her sister the ABCs. This would continue until her Granny came in and yelled at my mom for writing all over the walls. She was doing something right because she ended up receiving a Masters in Education from Vanderbilt University.

In my lifetime I have only ever known my mom's mother and step father, Donna and Ray McCord, who we refer to as MiMi and PawPaw. From what I have seen and heard about my real grandfather is that he and I have a lot of similar physical appearances, from height to weight to hairstyle. In my mind, he is a reckless cowboy, confused and alone. My mom shared how growing up he made her bag marijuana into penny, nickel and dime bags so he could sell them just to keep food on the table. She said he never had a phone or credit card or anything the government could trace. He would shoot anything living and eat anything he shot. My mom wasn't too keen but she did say you can't knock squirrel brains and eggs until you try it.

The last memory my mom has with her real dad is when he came to visit her after she had just given birth to me. My mom offered my grandfather the opportunity to stay on the condition that he stayed sober. The next night he went out, got drunk, came back, stole my mom's pain medication and left. No one in my family has seen him since.

The remaining memories with MiMi and PawPaw include crazy Thanksgivings like when MiMi refused to let my real grandfather in the house so he stood in the driveway, grilling whatever animal he had shot that day. MiMi ran outside with a shotgun and threatened to shoot him if he didn't leave. Other trips include going to Golden Corral, swinging on the tire swing outside their home in the deep woods of Tennessee, and "Oh, meet your cousin *[insert whatever name you can think of]*" more times than I can count. We call MiMi on the holidays and conversations usually go something like,

"Hi MiMi!"

"Hi boys! You sure are getting big! I saw your Mama's Facebook post. You know what else I saw on Facebook? An advertisement for a new grill. I was just telling PawPaw we need a new grill, but there ain't nothing wrong with the one I got now. I swear the government is listening to us through these damn cell phones. Actually PawPaw did burn himself one time. We had to take him to the hospital. Third trip to the hospital this week. Had to go in cuz I was having knee problems. These doctors don't know a thing. I swear they waste all that time and money on college. Not your Mama though. She's real smart. Thank Jesus for people like her."

Our family loves them as much as the rest of our family, but my mom yearned for adventure, love and new life.

Things in my Pocket

One of the first blessings in my life was the "adoption" of my mom into the Harris household. I put quotations around "adoption" because my mom was well into her twenties by this time and did not go through any legal adoption process. However, while going to Vanderbilt, my mom lived with Tom and Alene Harris. Tom was the lead professor of Biomedical Engineering and Alene was one of my mom's professors in Education at the University. During their time at Vanderbilt, Tom and Alene would provide housing for students going to school under the condition that they abide by their rules. So while she was in college, my mom was adopted into the customs of the Harris household; centered in Christ, education and discipline.

One story my mom shared of her time at the Harris household was when she went out, like many college kids do, and broke curfew that had been set by Tom and Alene. My mom says she had never seen them so angry. She looks back and is grateful for the loving discipline Tom and Alene showed because it was much different from her upbringing. That time with them was a pivotal point in my mom's life because the Harris Hotel is where my mom grew into the woman she is today. To this day, Tom and Alene are referred to as Granny and Papa by my brothers and I because of the bond we share with them as members of a family that love one another.

My dad, Matthew Otis Getchell, was a resident of Illinois, Indiana, Michigan, Missouri, Texas and every other state in the hit song "I've Been Everywhere" by Johnny Cash. He is the oldest of six children, two younger brothers and three younger sisters - Matt, Tonya, Debbie, Joe, John, and Kayla. My dad was raised by John and Gail Getchell. On my dad's side we call his parents Grandma and Grandpa.

Grandpa was deployed in Taiwan where he quickly fell in love while riding on the bus downtown. This love was short lived but tore Grandpa apart and took away his peace. Grandma said Grandpa prayed and prayed and prayed for an answer. Grandpa tells everyone that when he met Grandma, he had never felt more at peace and felt directly called to marry Grandma. He was so compelled that they were married two weeks after meeting. It was Grandma who mended his broken heart and gave him the peace he was looking for. Grandpa raised his family as an electrician and Grandma stayed at home with the kids, raising them in Christ-centered lives out in the middle of nowhere Missouri, where free time consisted of cave exploring and dirt bike riding. They never had insurance or investments, instead were the type of people who believed God would provide when the time was right.

Grandma has many stories but I will never forget the story she shared with me of the time she took her six kids to the community pool when they were all still young. Grandma recalls the anxiety and stress she felt trying to corral, discipline and get them all to listen to her. She was overwhelmed to the point where she sat down on a beach chair and cried right there in that community pool area. A random lady walked up to her and asked if she could pray for her. After praying for Grandma, the lady said

"Your offspring are going to do great things for the Kingdom of Heaven."

After returning home, Grandma prayed for clarity and pulled the classic Christian move, randomly flipping her Bible open with complete trust that God would speak to her. She looked down and read Isaiah 44:3,

Things in my Pocket

"For I will pour out water to quench your thirst and to irrigate your parched fields. And I will pour out my Spirit on your descendants, and my blessing on your children."

My dad's story is full of the evidence of God but it has no shortage of hardship. Being the oldest in a family with nothing, my dad had to grow up fast. If he wanted something, he had to work for it and get it himself. He stocked grocery stores so he could buy clothes, shoes and dirt bikes. My dad started his college career at DACC, Danville Area Community College in Illinois, home of the Jaguars. From there he transferred out of state to Michigan State University, where he earned a Bachelor's Degree in Construction Management. Like his father, my dad struggled when it came to solving the puzzle of love. At nineteen, my dad was engaged. The relationship did not last and he was lost pondering the question, "Who?".

While studying at Michigan State University, he lived with his aunt and uncle. My dad comes from a long line of work horses. My great grandfather came across the ocean from Germany, starting a new life as a brick mason with nothing but spit in his eye and grit in his teeth. My great uncle followed in his father's footsteps as a brick mason, my Grandpa was an electrician and my dad worked in the trades throughout his young adult life. Many of the same qualities and personality traits have passed down from generation to generation including the quiet, constant work day in and day out. Perrys and Getchells have a hard time *not* working. It is hard work laying brick everyday but they work hard and they work fast. While working for his uncle, my dad learned many things, including discipline and faith. One day he was working with his Uncle Bill when Dad stopped and asked,

"How will I know when I found the right woman for me?"

After a long pause to think, Uncle Bill shared the story of Isaac and Rebekah from the Bible. In the story, Isaac prays to God,

"Lord, show me who I am to marry."

The Lord tells Isaac that the woman who brings you water and brings water for your camels will be the person you are to marry. Now mind you, a camel can drink a bathtub of water. Multiply that by however many camels plus Isaac and you have a full day running back and forth from the well. To my understanding, the point of Uncle Bill sharing that story with Dad was that he would search for someone strong and independent, with discipline and able to raise a family.

Before even being born, a foundation of faith, discipline and strength was being built by two strong, independent oldest children in a rugged world with nothing but their own will to help them reach the goals they aspired to. I want to share with you the most shocking story, and my personal favorite to tell - the story of how my parents met.

A guy walks into a bar. More specifically, Matt Getchell and his brother Joe walk into Legends Corner located on Honky Tonk Highway in Nashville, Tennessee looking for an escape as they journey home from Florida back to Indiana. It just so happened that Theresa Medley's best friend, DeeDee, was scheduled to sing at Legends Corner that night. Theresa walks into Legends Corner, excited to listen to her friend sing classic country music hits from stars like Patsy Cline, Reba McEntire, and Martina McBride.

As the night progresses, Joe and DeeDee strike up a conversation at the bar. Obviously, I was not there but the way I picture the scene is Joe and

DeeDee sitting on bar stools and Matt and Theresa sitting on opposite sides of them. Eventually, Matt and Theresa get talking and in my mind the scene looks like Joe and DeeDee getting up to dance and the two of them left sitting there in awkward silence. Knowing my parents, I would bet money that my mom started the conversation between the two of them considering her outgoing personality and the fact that my dad had a girlfriend at that time. You heard me right.

Keep up here because this is where it gets interesting. Remember the story I told you of Uncle Bill's advice to my dad? The story of Isaac and Rebekah? Well after Uncle Bill gave that advice it became a running joke for Uncle Bill to try to persuade girls to offer my dad some water. Of course he never took it seriously and got annoyed with the joke over time, but something was different that night in Legends Corner. Somewhere between the small talk and conversation between the two, Theresa asked Matt if he wanted anything to drink. I don't know if he wasn't drinking that night or if he had already had enough, but he respectfully declined the offer. Theresa walked away and returned with a glass of water.

Many people have brought my dad numerous cups of water, but for some God given reason he took that offer of water in Legends Corner on Honky Tonk Highway in Nashville, Tennessee as a sign from God. Within one week, my dad called his girlfriend, broke up with her, asked my mom to be his girlfriend and went on to propose to her. From strangers to fiances in seven days. The next few weeks consist of my dad asking Tom and Alene Harris for my mom's hand in marriage and my mom telling John and Gail Getchell that she is going to marry their son. They dated long distance between

Indianapolis, Indiana and Nashville, Tennessee until they were able to plan the wedding and seal their wedding vows... Three short months in the summer of 1998. This story is too spontaneous, too creative, too outside social norms to make up. That is why it is my favorite to share.

Fast forward three years. At this point my dad had taken on a job in construction management that relocated my parents to the Bahamas - a perfect place for newly weds. My family has never taken a trip to the Bahamas and we joke that my parents are banned from ever going back there. While in the Bahamas, my mom worked with my dad as a secretary. The problem was my mom did not have a work visa and my dad's work visa did not permit him to work on the building he was working on. He had been transferred to another site after finishing the original building he was there for. They were detained and the funniest part of the whole thing is my mom's reaction to the situation.

My dad is a calm, quiet man who doesn't make a big scene even if it is appropriate. On the flip side, my mom will make a big scene even when it is *not* appropriate. She went on about how "We're U.S citizens and we have rights!" The best part was after hours of waiting in the detainment center with other illegal immigrants, my mom convinced security to let them order pizza while they waited. If I had to describe my parents with one story, it would be that one.

I drive my little, white Infiniti with pride. Pride in my upbringing. Pride in my ancestry. I think about my Granny and my mom, who drove this Infiniti before I did. I think about my dad when I drive my little, white Infiniti too fast, similar to how he drove at my age I'm sure. I get emotional thinking about my family when I drive my car, especially when I drive home.

Things in my Pocket

Home… My family has always struggled with this word. What is home? A place? A people? I have grown to define home as a feeling rather than a place or physical thing. Both my parents moved homes, school districts and states more times than they can remember. Because of this, they made it their priority to keep their kids in the same school district but I have still moved homes 6 times between elementary school and high school. The longest we ever lived in a house was maybe four years, until the one on Cedar Ridge where they lived for ten years, until 2022.

No matter where we moved, we stayed together. This feeling of home is felt whenever I drive. When I'm in my car, I think about my family. You may see me in a parking lot or driveway just sitting in my car. I sit in my car a lot. People have asked me why I sit in my car. My mom has gotten on to me for sitting in my car for too long and neglecting my chores. Nowadays, my car is sometimes my only space when I am alone. Alone to think, process, grieve. This is because my car makes me feel at home. Whenever I am anxious or homesick, I know I can reach in my pocket for my car keys. It is not about the destination, rather the journey as I drive.

Four

Notebook

I drove my car to Hope College, where I bought my first notebook as a way for me to stay organized. The first class I ever used my notebook in was in Journey to Leadership, focused on vocational discernment and using your strengths to create passions, and ultimately prepare you to graduate college. This first year seminar was taught by the Dean of Students, Richard Frost. Over time, my relationship with Dean Frost evolved from advisor to mentor to friend. I am grateful for my relationship with Dean Frost and the lessons he taught me in his class. Almost every time I see Dean Frost he asks me, "What are you doing to take care of Ethan?" Over time the answer to this question has developed with my maturity. As a freshman, I scoffed at this question.

"I'll take care of myself later!"

I would say with baggy eyes from four hours of sleep the night before. This question changed as I continued to transition through life. I understand the importance of self care and slowing down to prioritize the things that truly matter in life. Prioritizing the things that are life giving: Friends, family, health and prayer. Dean Frost has instilled a sense of self awareness in me that I continue to use to this day.

At his final end of year presentation before he retired, he reflected on his experience, the people that have impacted him, and the lessons he has learned. At the end of his presentation, he opened up the floor for questions from the audience. After a few questions, I raised my hand and asked, “What are you doing to take care of Richard?” The audience erupted in laughter. I am certain all of them have heard him ask them that question. So with my notebook, I write down the lessons from Richard Frost and I take care of myself.

My dad is a major influence in my life, especially in vocational discernment. Because my dad is in construction management, I thought I wanted to do the same thing when I graduate college. The problem is that Hope College does not have a construction management program. I knew I could still get into construction with a civil engineering degree or even an accounting degree, so after advice from my advisor, I decided to pursue engineering. The summer after my freshman year, my dad helped me get an internship with Wieland Construction, a private general contractor. I lived in an apartment in Kalamazoo, MI and worked on site of one of the largest paper factory construction sites in the United States. Because of the work ethic instilled in me from my dad, when I finished an assignment, I went and asked what the next thing to do was. In the end, this led to them running out of projects for me to do so they gave me a buggy and a fifty gallon tank of water and had me drive around the site watering the plants. Even though the work was mundane, I am grateful for the relationships I built that summer.

I knew what my strengths were: significance, competition, focus, futuristic and learner. I also knew I had a gift for reading, writing and public speaking. But in my mind, I didn't see a reality where I could make money doing those things. I thought I needed to spend my time growing my weaknesses, such as math, science and STEM in general. I decided to pursue an engineering degree freshman year. As a result, my first year at Hope College was the worst I had ever done in terms of GPA in all my years of schooling.

I constantly called my family, expressing the difficulty of the subject matter and my lack of it clicking in my mind. Ultimately, my parents wanted me to do what I wanted to do and if it wasn't engineering that was fine with them. I had to shift my perspective from one that looks at growing my weaknesses to one that focuses on developing my strengths. I switched to business with the mindset that I could still get into construction management with a business accounting degree. Unfortunately, I was still left unfulfilled. The classes were hard and I wasn't loving the material. However, as part of the business major, students are required to take public presentations. So in the spring of 2021, I started public presentations with Professor Rob Pocock.

I knew Professor Pocock looked familiar but I couldn't figure out why at first. Then I remembered student admitted day during the spring of my senior year, when Professor Pocock was the keynote speaker in the Bultman Student Center Great Room. Professor Pocock was an intimidating introduction to college life because he set the bar high. He talked about his three main points with descriptive finger gestures, and called us to come up with our action plans with SMART goals and objectives for our time in college. I didn't even know what I wanted to eat for lunch that day, let alone my plans for the rest of college. Professor Pocock stood out because he didn't just stand up on the stage and talk at us. He walked between the tables, engaged with the audience and put on a show as much as a seminar. His personality and engagement stood out when I was in high school, and it stood out in his public presentation course.

By the time Spring 2021 came around I was in my third semester of college and I did what every rebellious twenty year old does. I grew out my hair. My mom told me how as a child, I would love to play with her hair. It didn't matter if I was eating, napping or sitting there, I always had a hand twirling my mom's hair. This habit never left and with long hair especially, I found myself constantly twirling my hair. My mom hates this habit and says I won't ever get a job if I don't quit twirling my hair. It has yet to stop me.

One day in class I was sitting there twirling my hair as I always do, listening to Professor Pocock give a lecture on conveying "clear, concise and specific" information in a speech. Mid lecture he stops, looks at me, and tells me to stop twirling my hair. He called me out in front of the whole class. I was not embarrassed, but I was shocked. Those who know Professor Pocock would not be surprised by this. After class, I went up to him and told him how my mom tells me the same thing. I see a lot of similarities between my mom and Professor Pocock as two people with gifts and passions for communication. When I got back to my dorm, I told my mom this story. She asked for

Professor Pocock's email so she could write him a thank you letter. I did so and went back to my studies.

The next class period, Professor Pocock came up to me before class and expressed his gratitude for the letter my mom wrote him. In the letter, she shared how it was difficult for her oldest child to be out of the house, living independently, and honestly not communicating the best. He told me that for the rest of the semester he would give me one point extra credit if I could prove that I had a conversation with my mom that week. Every week after that, I would come into class and show Professor Pocock a call or text string between my mom and me. Throughout my time in college, Professor Pocock has been a professor, advisor, mentor and friend to me. This story is a testament to Professor Pocock, the Communication Department and Hope College in general.

Public Presentations required us to meet once a week to give presentations based on the prompt assigned for the week, and to come prepared to take a quiz based on the book work assigned for that week. The class has a lot of creative liberty, so I jumped on the opportunity to go above and beyond.

The assigned presentation for the week was an occasional speech that either introduces, thanks or commemorates an individual or group. As a member of Student Congress, I saw how much they have done for Hope through the presidential election, racial disparity and a pandemic. I chose to honor them and thank them for the work they have done in order to pay them respect and also inform the audience what exactly Student Congress has done for them.

Things in my Pocket

We are taught in class how to give a speech, starting with an anchor position, having three areas of the stage to move from that coordinate with the main points while using descriptive hand gestures and vocal variety to enhance the presentation. Speech after speech, students got up and gave their presentations on various people and topics, yet each one was as predictable as the last. "By a show of hands how many of you have ___?" "Today I am going to show you ___." The repetition and monotony was grueling. When it was my turn to present, I made it my goal to think outside the box and creatively communicate my ideas in a way that was fresh and exciting.

Instead of getting up in front of the audience and starting my presentation the same way everyone else did, I pulled up a chair and sat in front of them with my leg crossed over the other, twirling my thumbs. My professor gave me a concerned look that quickly shifted to amazement as I began. "Many people believe this is what student congress does… sit there twirling their thumbs." Then I stood, slammed the chair back against the wall and continued with, "however, student congress STANDS for so much more." Dramatic, I know.

When I look at my notebook, I remember all of the presentation brainstorming done in that book. I remember the many meeting notes from conversations with Professor Pocock. I would go into his office and ask for names of people to network with. Name after name, he would put me in contact with alumni and professionals. I am grateful for my relationship with Professor Pocock. I am grateful for the advice he has given me, but more importantly the space he has given me to run with my creativity.

A core memory of Professor Pocock was in the spring of 2021 when I was applying to the Hope College Business Department Baker Scholar program. This is the elite group within the business department that offers contacts to alumni, professional development and trips during breaks. Professor Pocock helped me prepare for my interview. We spent a lot of hours preparing and I really wanted to get in.

Unfortunately, I did not get in. I thought I was okay when I received the news, not too emotional. I told myself I didn't care. It wasn't until I returned to Professor Pocock's office that I fell apart. I felt like I had let myself and him down. However, that painful moment was pivotal to the ultimate success of my college career. After giving me a space to grieve, Professor Pocock asked me what I wanted to get out of Baker Scholars. I told him that I wanted student engagement, professional development and community involvement. He asked if I had ever heard of Lambda Pi Eta, the Communication Honor Society. I had not, and he suggested that I accept my invitation to join my junior year and step into leadership to create these things that I wanted. That fall, I was inducted into the honor society and I became president of the organization.

At that time, LPH was not at peak performance. Membership was low and the campus didn't even know about this group. Professor Pocock was the advisor of the group, and we spent the first year just analyzing the problems of the group. I served as president of LPH for two years under the mentorship of Professor Pocock. LPH became my baby and I am very proud of their growth and success today. We hosted events with alumni like John McFarlin, Hope College Board of Trustee member and inductee to the Michigan Journalism

Hall of Fame. I enjoy flipping through my notebook and reading about the frustrations and struggles of the past and contrasting them with the successes and wins of the present.

Inside this notebook you will find notes from all of my internships. After my sophomore year, I worked in Traverse City doing property management and real estate investment with a developer I met through my relationship with Wieland. This experience spurred my curiosity to pursue development in some capacity. I spent most of the summer sweeping dust, picking up dog poop and planting flowers, but I could not complain about being in a new apartment complex in Traverse City. My mentors even let me sit in on meetings and helped me learn the financial terminology. I continued to have lots of conversations about this career pathway, and the advice I received was to start in real estate brokerage to learn the market. So I started cold calling commercial real estate firms until I connected with Duke Suwyn with Advantage Commercial Real Estate.

Advantage didn't have any official summer internship opportunities available but they were willing to make one for me as a research analyst for the summer. I am very grateful for the team at Advantage for taking me under their wing and teaching me about commercial real estate. That summer, I filled my notebook with notes, questions, words I didn't understand, and names of people I had talked to.

In the fall of my senior year, I made it my goal to have a job before I walked across the stage at graduation. I joined the Econ Club in Grand Rapids, where I continued to network and talk to professionals in commercial real estate. I was talking to every big commercial real estate firm in Grand Rapids:

Colliers, JLL, Bradley Company, NAI, and CBRE. By the spring, I narrowed it down to Bradley Company and CBRE. I visited their offices and met their employees. I could see myself at either company.

That spring semester, I was sitting in the student center studying and I saw retired Dean Frost walk into the building. We made eye contact and both of us lit up. I jumped up and we hugged. He asked me what I was planning to do after graduation. I told him I was planning on going into commercial real estate. Because he was my advisor freshman and sophomore year, he knows that I am always scheming and have ideas on the back burner, so he asked me, "What's your crazy idea?"

Up until that point, I had never verbalized it, but I wanted to go to grad school so I could earn my counseling license and work with marginalized communities. I was trying to fit this desire to help others into commercial real estate with the idea that I could develop housing for low income people and families to live in. However, I found that there was such a chase, such a self interest mentality in commercial real estate, that I struggled to see the reality of me helping other people significantly.

After expressing this to Dean Frost, he gave me the kick in the pants that I needed. "Then do it! It's not too late. Just go talk to someone." So I did. I talked to the Director of Counseling and Psychological Services at Hope, who told me this dream was realistic and a needed one. I talked to Dale Austin, who helped me navigate possible grad school paths. At first, I was thinking about a psychology track, but there were too many prerequisites in the way and I didn't want to come back to Hope to take more classes. However, we landed on the Social Work track because there were no prerequisites in the way and I could apply right away. From there I went and talked to Dr. Feaster in the Social Work department. His conversation affirmed and inspired what I wanted to do.

He brought my whole college career full circle. He explained how similar social work is to engineering. Engineering is an interdisciplinary field that pulls from physics, chemistry, biology and math. Social work is an interdisciplinary field that pulls from economics, communication, psychology, etc. Engineering creates, evolves and fixes the material world. Social work creates, evolves, and fixes human nature. Instead of viewing my business and communication degree as putting me behind in social work, he helped me see it as being specialized with a unique ability to help people with my degree.

In February of my senior year, I pivoted. I called Bradley Company and CBRE and let them know what I was doing. I called my parents and told them what I wanted to do. They were all supportive and encouraged me to pursue this journey. The next step was applying to grad schools. I applied to the University of Michigan, North Carolina Chapel Hill, Catholic University of America, and University of Denver. The craziest part is that I was accepted into every program I applied to. I don't say this to boast, but to share the testament of following what I believed to be God's calling on my life, and his providence through opening doors for me.

I bought a notebook when I got to college. This notebook has helped me remember people, remember lessons I have learned, prepare for job interviews, and most recently prepare for grad school interviews. If you had told the Ethan buying this notebook freshman year what he would be doing after he graduated, he would not have believed you. I am grateful for all the names in this book. All the mentors who answered my questions, all the professionals who took a chance on me, and all the people who have encouraged me to not settle on what is comfortable, but chase my dreams.

Three months after pivoting from the path I had started down four years ago, I am proud to announce I am headed to the University of Michigan to pursue my Master's in Social Work so that I can become a clinical counselor. I will take the lessons with me that I have learned. I will continue to have the same hunger for knowledge and desire to help others. And, I will need a new notebook.

Things in my Pocket

Five

Sunglasses

I have multiple pairs of sunglasses. I have the cheap pair that I wear whenever I mow the lawn or have yard work to do. I have a pair of Ray Bans that I like to wear to the beach. I also have a very special pair of sunglasses. On my 21st birthday, my brother Haden surprised me with a nice pair of aviators that he bought while on a trip in Europe. At first I was apprehensive because I did not consider myself someone who wears aviators. However, they started to come in handy in the fall of my senior year.

One of the reasons my dad moved to Michigan was to pursue aviation at Michigan State University so that he could go into the Airforce. After an injury left him unable to join the military, he switched to construction management. He talks about going back and getting his pilot's license, but he encouraged me to give it a try as well. In the fall of my senior year, I had the opportunity to pursue this passion. It just so happens that one of my best friend's dad is a flight instructor. Mark Bos offered to take me on a discovery flight to see if a pilot's license would be something I would be interested in pursuing.

Things in my Pocket

There is an airport in Holland called Tulip City airport. After class one day, I drove ten minutes south to the little, non-towered airport. I met Mark in the lobby and he gave me the debrief of what to expect. We were going to take off, head south for about ten miles, and return to the airport in a rectangular pattern. As we walked through the hangar, we walked past these big, amazing jets. Dual prop, turbo engines that seat ten people in the cabins. White leather interior with gold around the edges. We walked past the single engine jets that were a little bit smaller, a little bit older. Could still hold 4-6 people. I got more and more excited, feeling the pair of sunglasses weighing in my pocket.

We walked around the corner to the plane we had reserved. It was a red and white Cessna 152 single prop engine that seats two people. We climbed in, sitting shoulder to shoulder. I reached in my pocket and pulled out my aviators. I put them on, followed by a headset that we use to communicate in the air. I felt like I was on the set of *Top Gun*. We taxi'd to the runway and prepared to take off. Mark was communicating to the other pilots in the area, and it felt like a different language trying to understand what they were saying. We went through the run-up checklist and we were ready to fly.

I remember sitting there in the plane preparing to take off with six thousand feet of runway ahead of me, just sweating. Mark gave it full throttle, looked for all green indicators, and slowly started to pull back. Before I knew it, we were in the air. It went from terrifying to peaceful quickly. Being in Holland, we are right on the coast of Lake Michigan. The coastal view with the sun starting to set was a beautiful sight to see. I've been in Holland for years and in Michigan my whole life, but I had never seen Lake Michigan from that angle.

Mark asked me if I wanted to take control of the plane. It went from terrifying, to beautiful, back to terrifying. He let go of his controls and my sweaty hands grabbed the yoke. It took me a minute to understand the feeling of the third dimension of altitude, but I adjusted and the fear turned back into excitement. In a car, you have two dimensions to control: speed and direction. You push the gas pedal to speed up and the brake to slow down. You turn the steering wheel left to go left, and right to go right. In a plane, you have the same steering to go left and right. There is even a similar throttle to speed up and slow down, however it is a metal bar that you push in with your hand to speed up and pull out to slow down.

The third dimension, and most complicated to overcome, is altitude. Instead of a stational steering wheel, the yoke turns left and right, but also pushes and pulls in and out. Pushing the yoke points the nose down and pulling the yoke makes the nose point up. To make things even more complicated, there are pedals on the floor. Except these pedals have nothing to do with speed, like they do in a car. These pedals control the rudder and control the plane's yaw. This yaw is the angle a plane will have based on the influence of wind. You use the pedals to adjust the rudder to correct for wind.

Don't even get me started about stalling out. If you start flying too steep, you begin to cut off the airflow over the plane. When there is no air flowing over the plane, your plane forgets how to fly and starts falling out of the sky. Best case is prevention, but you can recover from a stall rather simply by pointing the nose back down to recover air flow. Mark is telling me this information on our first flight and it is all going in one ear and out the other.

Things in my Pocket

After the discovery ride, I was hooked. Mark became my flight instructor and I bought Sporty's online ground school. In order to get my VFR license (Visual Flight Rules) I have to have forty-ish hours of flight time, complete the ground schooling, which takes about 30 hours, take the ground test, pass a check ride, and pass a medical exam. During the fall, I slowly started collecting hours flying with Mark. Over winter break during my senior year, I completed Sporty's online ground school. In the spring, I started flying more consistently and things started coming together.

Each step is terrifying, until it becomes routine over time and I look back and think, why was I so scared? I remember the first time Mark let me take off. It was the same six thousand feet of runway, except this time I was in control. I lined it up straight, gave it full throttle, and started pulling back until I was no longer on the ground. To this day, every time I take off and push that throttle all the way in, my heart starts pumping and the adrenaline kicks in.

The next step was learning the Comm/Nav. Learning the language of pilots. Whether it was obtaining weather, listening to control towers, or other pilots in the air, they speak in numbers and random words that make no sense to the uneducated ear. Fortunately, at an uncontrolled airport with no tower traffic control, I am free to make mistakes without too much consequence. The general outline for communication when speaking is "Who you're talking to, who you are, where you are, what you want to do, and who you're talking to again". When flying around the airport in Holland, this looks like, "Holland traffic, this is Cessna seven bravo sierra, departing runway 26, staying in the pattern, Holland traffic". I started by flying around, repeating this communication based on where I was, talking to no one specifically. Over time, I learned what the numbers represented and how to say letters when speaking pilot lingo. I became able to speak to tower control and other pilots.

The hardest part, and part I am currently learning is how to land. There are so many moving pieces as you try to control pitch for speed and power for height. You have one hand on the yoke and one hand on the throttle. You are using the pedals to keep the plane straight as the wind tries to push you off course. And then the key is learning when to flare. As you approach the runway in a floating tin can, going about 80 miles per hour towards the ground, you have to time it just right and pull back on the yoke to take out the energy and land smoothly. If you flare too early, you lose your energy and fall out of the sky, landing hard. If you flare too late, you don't take out the necessary energy and you land too hot, leaving the potential for a crash.

Whether you are taking off, cruising around, or landing, you have to stay calm. There are checklists and processes for any situation. The worst mistake you can make is freaking out or rushing any of the checklists or processes. Flying has taught me a lot about discipline and attention to detail. There is a preflight checklist, a taxi checklist, a run up checklist, a climbing checklist, a cruising checklist, a landing checklist, and a checklist for anything else you can imagine. The pop culture pilot who walks up, jumps in the plane and takes off is not exactly accurate. But the aviators are still just as cool.

Things in my Pocket

Six

Airpods

In my pocket, I carry a set of Airpods with me. I put them in when I study and I put them in when I go to the gym. These airpods remind me of my time in sports. In middle school, I played football, basketball and baseball because that was what all the "cool" kids did at my school, even though I sucked at those sports. In high school, I grew into myself and stopped caring as much about what other people thought. I still played football the fall of my freshman year of high school. However, after the season ended a friend of mine, and senior on the wrestling team, told me I should join the wrestling team because they needed someone my size. I didn't like basketball anyway, so I agreed to try out for the team. I was intimidated by the experience of the other wrestlers on the team and the intensity of the practices, but the coaches did their best to make the process enjoyable by starting me on JV. Soon after the season started, Mark Holdren pulled me aside and told me how they had a hole in their varsity lineup, specifically at 112 pounds. I weighed about 130 pounds at the time and had never cut weight before. Still, the competitive side of me agreed to work on getting to that weight so I could wrestle on varsity and earn my varsity letter as a freshman.

I successfully cut to 112 pounds my freshman year and earned a spot on the varsity lineup. As excited as I was about this accomplishment, I didn't fully understand the learning curve from wrestling on JV to wrestling on varsity. That season I think my record was four wins and twenty six losses. Even though I spent most of that season losing, I was proud to be on varsity and proud of the little wins to support my team. One example was when we were wrestling Lakewood High School at the Michigan Team District Finals match. How wrestling works is there are 14 weight classes and each weight has a wrestler who competes against the person on the other team in the same weight class. This meet started at 125 lbs so I was the last match to go. There is a point system award based on how you beat the other person. If you beat them by getting more takedowns you get four points. If you beat them extensively it is called a technical fall or "tech" and you get five points. If you pin your opponent, you get six points. When it came time for me to compete, our team was winning by 5 points. All I had to do was not get pinned.

A wrestling match is three rounds, two minutes each. The longest six minutes of my life. My opponent was significantly better than me, but I did not want to let my team down. I fought hard and spent the majority of that match planking on my head to keep my shoulders from touching the mat and getting pinned. I lost the match, but I was proud of that match. My team won and I was celebrated. My mom recalls being anxious, on the edge of her seat the entire match. She said it was hard to watch her baby struggling out there on the mat. I was just happy I didn't get pinned. This memory inspired my passion for wrestling and led to me wrestling all four years in high school.

Soccer, wrestling, and golf. I played soccer for the conditioning in preparation for wrestling season, and I played golf as a break from a strenuous wrestling season. After my sophomore year of high school I went to JRobinson intensive wrestling camp in Iowa. This camp was ten days of wrestling, with four workouts a day. We woke up in the morning and did a run or lift, we had a light and a heavy wrestling practice in the afternoon, and another lift or run in the evening. Wake up, workout, eat, workout, eat, workout, eat, workout, sleep. Day after day. On the tenth day we were given the task to go on a run. We had the choice to do a nine mile version or a twelve mile version. This choice was to test our mental strength. I ran with my buddy, Owen Guilford, and we chose to do the twelve mile run. Most people did. I had never run that far in my entire life, but I learned a lot about myself. I put my airpods in and set off. We completed the run in an hour and a half and I cried tears of joy having completed the JRob ten day intensive camp.

My saving grace during that trip was music. The camp was led by J Robinson, Iowa wrestling coach and Olympic wrestling coach in his day. Every day he had a different lesson to share. We had a book that we had to fill out and they checked it everyday. If we didn't fill out the journal for that day, we all had to do push ups. One day, after a hard wrestling workout, Jay gathered us up and shared one of his lessons with us. He said that we should all have one song that gets our adrenaline pumping. He said that every day he drives into practice, he listens to "Poker Face" by Lady Gaga. For some reason, that song gets his blood pumping and gets him ready to go every day.

I took this lesson to heart, and my friends all know the one song that gets my adrenaline pumping whenever I listen to it. That song is "Imma Be" by the Black Eyed Peas. I could be having the worst day ever, no motivation to workout, and listening to that song will get me moving. My brother knows this so he will take advantage of this by coming into my room when I am napping and play the song to get me to workout with him. I can throw in my airpods, crank up some Black Eyed Peas, and be ready to take on anything.

After I graduated high school and hung up the head gear, I still craved competition and that adrenaline rush that comes from wrestling. I found a boxing gym called Sakwando in Holland, MI. This gym is a small, mom and pop shop with old weights, a few bags hanging up, and one boxing ring in the corner. This gym is the definition of grit. The coach is an older, black gentleman who is very fit for his age. He and his wife run the gym and he trains anyone from kids to adults, one on one to classes. I called the gym and asked if I could come in for an introductory lesson. From the moment I stepped through that door, I fell in love with that gym.

There is no hype, no speakers, no funny business. We warm up by running around the parking lot. On longer runs, Coach would hop on his bike and make me run in front of him. Coach took me under his wing and trained me one on one. Over time, I started to help coach the kids' class and met some amazing people. I never competed officially, but he trained me to compete. He put me in the ring and let me spar with some of his semi pros. I was knocked down, knocked out, and beat up like never before. But underneath all of it was respect and appreciation for the sport.

Coach is a unique individual. He is passionate about his craft. He has a deep voice, and he always wears a mask so it’s a deep muffled voice. He always wears a beanie on his head, a black Sakwando boxing tee shirt with a white long sleeve underneath, and a white wife beater tank top underneath that. Along with the mask, he wears blue latex gloves, black sweatpants and sneakers. When I walk in it's always "Hey! There's the super star." He describes himself as a boxer, an entrepreneur, and a motivational speaker. He coaches in metaphors. "When you box, you gotta stand like you're standing on a surfboard." "You gotta be like a boat floating in the water, rocking with the waves and adjusting to the changes." "Boxing is like making sweet love to a woman. You gotta know the right moves and know when to use 'em." I could go on and on.

Coach also loves music. Whenever we worked out, he played '80s music from his little Harman Kardon speaker. Because of him, I fell in love with working out with Michael Jackson. To this day, when I workout with my airpods in, I think of Coach Sakwam whenever Michael Jackson comes on.

After boxing for about a year, I moved to Traverse City for the summer after my sophomore year to work a property management internship. While up there, I wanted to continue my boxing training so I wouldn't get rusty. I couldn't find a solo boxing gym, but I found this Warrior Combat Academy. At this gym they train a different martial art each day of the week. Monday is kickboxing. Tuesday is jiu jitsu. Wednesday is boxing. Thursday is muay thai. Friday is MMA. Saturday is wrestling. I started just going to the boxing classes, but my curiosity peaked at the thought of learning some other martial arts. That summer I was introduced to kickboxing, jiu jitsu, and muay thai while I sharpened my boxing and wrestling skills.

At the end of the summer, I overheard a conversation from the coaches and owners of the gym. They were putting on an in-house exhibition

MMA fight with multiple weight classes. The competition was already set, but I heard them talking about needing another fighter because they had a drop out at around 165 lbs. Conveniently, that is almost exactly what I weighed so I thought about it for approximately 30 seconds and then chirped up and said I was willing to compete if they needed someone. They were excited and more than willing to have me participate. Before I knew what I was getting myself into, I was signed up for a cage fight. Leading up to the fight, I was more disciplined and regimented, treating it like I was preparing for a big wrestling match. Except this time my opponent could throw knees or elbows or punches.

The day of the fight came around and my friends Emily and Kennedy came up to watch. I warmed up for a while, airpods in, listening to "Imma Be". They brought me to the back, wrapped my hands and gave me a pair of six ounce gloves and sent me on my way. I saw my opponent, who was a shorter, stockier guy about my age with a few tattoos on his body. Next thing I knew, I was walking into the cage and they were locking the door behind me. The only way out was through fighting this opponent. The ref was explaining the rules but all I could think about was how crazy this all was. Two guys, shirtless, with tiny gloves, getting ready to pound the snot out of each other with a crowd of people watching and cheering as their entertainment.

We bumped fists and the fight began. All of the new techniques I learned that summer went out the window as soon as this guy threw a kick at my face. I stuck with my bread and butter: boxing and wrestling. I didn't throw any kicks and I didn't take the fight to the ground because I didn't want to risk getting choked out on the floor.

The first round was slow. I was nervous and I was reading my opponent. I could tell I was a much better boxer than he was, and I also saw how he threw slopping kicks. He would land off balance and sometimes sideways to me. I was connecting punches and dominated most of the fight. The second round, I got more confident. When he threw a sloppy kick, I charged in with punches and wrapped him up with my wrestling background. Without thinking, I lifted him and suplexed him on his head. This felt illegal because it's illegal in wrestling. But the crowd loved it. In the third round, I connected more punches and my opponent's coach kept yelling "He's a boxer, he's a boxer!" Like, oh no you found out my secret. There was nothing he could do about it. Late in the third round, my opponent threw another sloppy kick, I once again slipped in and wrapped him up, lifted him, and dropped him on his head. This time I spun around and kneed him in the head. He didn't move after that. The crowd erupted and my hand was lifted. I had won my first, and last, MMA fight by TKO.

When I hold my airpod case or put in my airpods, I am reminded of the blood, sweat and tears I have shed in my athletic career. I am grateful for all of my coaches and sparring partners who have invested time and energy into me. Coaches are so instrumental in developing young people into who they will become. They instilled work ethic, discipline and my competitive nature in me.

It is important to take care of your physical health. I appreciate eating healthy and being disciplined in what I consume. It is also important to be self aware. I stopped fighting because I found myself becoming aggressive. Nothing extreme, but in my free time, I would want to wrestle or fight my friends. I would get antsy for practice, and need to hit something for my outlet. This form of an outlet didn't feel the healthiest to me, so I pivoted. My senior year I started rock climbing. I bought a membership, some shoes, some chalk and started climbing. The best part is my friends also got into climbing. Jared, Luke, Haden and I started a group chat and texted the group whenever we wanted to go climbing.

Climbing is unique because it is competitive, yet also chill. You compete with yourself to see what the hardest route is you can climb. There is also competition among my friends and I to see who can climb the hardest route. And yet, it is at your own pace. We sit around, talk about life, eat snacks, and climb walls when we want to. The community is great, too. It is surrounded by the idea of learning. Learning the best techniques. Learning new places to climb. Talking about previous trips and experiences. It is a great combination of working out and enjoying the outdoors.

Sometimes I will go to the climbing gym alone, throw in my airpods, and listen to music while I climb. Whether I am climbing a wall, hiking a mountain, hitting balls on a range, or performing some other kind of workout, I have my airpods with me to listen to music. I have my Black Eyed Peas and my Michael Jackson. I have my song that hypes me up, and my song I can't listen to without crying. I think everyone should have those songs for them. Someone once told me that everyone has a book, a poem, and a song in them. Who knows? Maybe after this I'll write a song. I doubt anyone will want to hear me sing it.

Seven

Pen

Consider this the rolling credits of my book. Equivalent to the 14 minutes and 35 second song "Note to Self" by J. Cole in his album *2014 Forest Hills Drive.* I carry a gold, screw top pen in my pocket, and it reminds me of friendship because it was gifted to me by one of my best friends, Emily Damstra. This same friend encouraged me to write this book. Friendship is a necessary component of life. As humans, we were created to be social creatures and depend on others throughout our life. This chapter is a rolling credits of the friendships that stand out in my life. These people are reliable, accountable, and some of the best friends I could ask for in life. I apologize in advance if I do not single you out specifically. Just because you are not included here does not mean we are not friends. I am blessed to say that if I tried to include every friend I have in this chapter, this book would be thicker than a bible.

Things in my Pocket

I may not know who I am going to marry yet, but I know exactly who my groomsmen will be. Of course, Haden will be my best man. Haden is my best friend in the whole wide world. Happens to be a fortunate coincidence that he is also my brother. We are so different, but also so similar. People sometimes think we are twins. We are both about six foot and weigh about 185 pounds. We argue and we fight, but it's because we are so similar. We are competitive and we challenge each other. But we also know when to slow down and comfort each other. We are not afraid to have hard conversations with each other and I trust Haden with information about me that no one else knows. I could not ask for a better brother/best friend package. I wrote Haden a letter that he has not seen yet. It sums up our relationship well.

"Dear Haden,

Quite honestly, I don't know what I would do without you. While in Alaska they asked us who we are thankful for. They asked us who we look up to and who our best friend is. My answer to all of these questions is you. I am thankful to have a brother like you. You are a model of pushing the pace and challenging yourself. When times are challenging, I catch myself asking, what would Haden do? What would Haden say? You balance growth with rest. You have a gift of connecting with people through servant leadership. It took me a long time and some painful experiences to learn servant leadership and I think it comes quite naturally to you. Your ability to know what someone needs and comfort them while still encouraging them to grow is so mature.

I think of my favorite memories in life, and you are there. I think of times when I have experienced the most joy, and you are there. My hope as you transition into this next season of life is that you continue to be a servant leader who puts others first and challenges them to grow. There will be beauty and there will be pain, but I hope you know I am someone you can always go to. I am very thankful for you.

Love,

Ethan"

Not in any particular order, the rest of my groomsmen will be Parker Bos, Will Harahan, Jared Poliskey, and Luke Shoemaker. I have been independently friends with these guys for years. I am grateful that in my senior year of college, there was a collision of worlds and all of the guys I call my best friends started hanging out and being friends with each other. What I love about my friend group is that they are all so different. We can vary in schools of thought, argue, debate, and still understand that we fall under the same umbrella of brotherhood and love.

Jared Poliskey and I met my sophomore year at Hope (in my man bun phase) when I was his residential assistant in the dorms. We lived in Phelps Hall and we bonded over our passions to be healthier people. He was working out a lot and I was trying to workout more. Jared and another friend of mine, Alec Kowalski, convinced me to do Exodus 90 with them. Through this season of prayer and sacrifice, we supported each other and held each other accountable. We shared stories and were vulnerable with each other. Since sophomore year, Jared and I have gone on many adventures together, like our trip to Alaska when we climbed mountains together.

One specific example that exemplifies Jared and I's relationship was when we were hiking in Alaska. One note is that I do not have any hiking or climbing experience. Jared has been hiking and climbing for years. When we were in Alaska, we went to several national parks and "bagged" multiple peaks as Jared would say. One day, our group went to Independence Mine State Historical Park in Palmer, AK. We were given the freedom to roam around and explore. One group ventured into the abandoned mines. Another group sought higher elevation. Jared saw a peak up ahead of us and determined that he was going to bag it. I followed behind him and at first thought this was a realistic goal. However, I became very aware of how icy and snowy the mountain was as we got higher in elevation. Mind you, this is not a well beaten path that we are walking up, rather a face of a mountain with blueberry patches that we clung to and crawled up. I grew more and more weary about the idea of climbing up, and then back down this rough terrain. Jared continued to reassure me that we were "almost to the top." I wasn't buying it.

One of our advisors, Matt Mulder, walked to the edge of the base of the mountain we were attempting to climb and yelled up to us if we needed anything. We said we were good and encouraged him to join us. He started crawling up behind us, but lost his grip and started rolling back down the mountain. When I saw that I freaked out. If I lost my grip and rolled from our height, I would get seriously hurt. We asked Matt if he was okay and he reassured us he was alright, but he wasn't going to join us. We thought we were about 75% there and we asked Matt how close to the top we looked.

"Ehhh, you look about a quarter of the way there."

Great. It's getting steeper and we're not even close.

Jared was still giddy about his adventure. We continued climbing until we reached a point where we had to do some traversing. The way up was unavailable and the only option to continue was to traverse left over a sheet of ice and snow. We did not have any proper equipment. I was climbing in my Brooks sneakers. Jared asked me to hand him a rock and he proceeded to punch into the ice with the rock and use it as a hand grip. He kicked his feet into the ice and called it good. He wanted me to follow in his tracks. I was very hesitant because I knew slipping and falling meant injury. However, I said a prayer to God and mustered all the energy I had to follow this crazy friend of mine.

There was a point where I felt like I was climbing vertically up the mountain. Jared says I was being dramatic but it was steep enough where if you stood straight up, you would lose your balance and fall. I was hugging the mountain for dear life. In a final act of persuasion, I convinced Jared to head back down the mountain. He was disappointed and even recorded a video of me saying we were going down so that he would have proof it was my fault we went back down and not his. Jared may be sad we did not bag that peak, but I am grateful to be alive.

We bagged other peaks together. During our trip, we went to Denali National Park and spent three days climbing Mount Margaret. We climbed to the top, spent the night on the top of the peak, and then climbed down the next day. I carried the gold, screw top pen with me on that trip and journaled my experience at the top. Our advisor, Timothy Schoonveld, encouraged us to write letters to people we appreciate while on the trip. Besides the letter to Haden, I wrote a letter to Jared on that mountain and I have never shared it with him. I wrote:

"Dear Jared,

What a ride it has been. I cannot think of a time before you were in my life. It feels like you have always been there. Your friendship, accountability, and outlook on life have shaped me into the person I am today. Climbing Mount Margaret was an accurate metaphor for our relationship. Together, our friendship is founded on the pursuit of holiness. I am thankful for what you have taught me about living a life that confuses people. I am thankful for our accountability and vulnerability. I prayed for years that God would give me that kind of accountability and I truly believe you are an answer to those prayers.

When we were climbing, the same word kept coming to mind when I thought about you. Pioneer. As far as leadership personalities, they say pioneers are the most rare, with only four percent of people having that trait. I admire that about you and I pray you embrace that for good. You will accomplish any goal you set for yourself. You are strong and independent. My prayer for you is that, like Paul in Second Corinthians Chapter Twelve, you will accept, appreciate, and share your weaknesses as often as you share your strengths. I am excited for our next adventure together.

Love,

Ethan"

Parker Bos! When I see that name I smile. When anyone sees Parker, they smile. That is the presence Parker Bos gives. I stand on my soapbox and preach being emotional and being healthy men, and Parker lives it. We have laughed together, we have cried together. We have shot guns together, and we have talked about our feelings together. I swear Parker wears his Getchell Brothers sweatshirt everyday. I love Parker like he is my own blood. He hugs my mom when he sees her and he gets my dad riled up talking about hunting trips. When we were in the heat of our business days together, we would spend hours sitting in the car together talking about life. Parker loves his family. He loves his grandparents. He has a tattoo on his forearm in honor of his late grandfather. We can talk and play and goof off, but we can also work together. Parker understands work ethic and he understands people. Wherever he goes, whatever he does, Parker will be successful. Not because he is the best or brightest, but because he cares the most about people. I have first hand experienced the love that Parker has and he is an inspiration to me to show more love. When we end our calls together, we always get into the same argument.

"Ok bye, love you"

"Love you more"

"Love you most"

"Love you mostestestestestestest"

"Ok you win"

They say iron sharpens iron, and that is what comes to mind when I think of Luke Shoemaker. Luke Shoemaker is a sharp man. Ran cross country most of his life, including college where he was the captain of the team. Biochemistry something or other major going on to Emery for grad school. I just tell people he's a scientist. Luke is the kind of guy where when we are sitting around he goes, "let's have a deep conversation about something." The problem is he knows so much about so many things. Whenever we have a conversation or debate something, I know I have to come prepared. Everytime we do, I leave questioning myself and I appreciate this because I have to go back and do more research. Luke does not just accept anything. However, he respects effort. He will agree to disagree if I am talking sense. He will run with me if he knows I am trying. He makes the most out of life. Luke also has a lot of love. He has the unique ability to love anyone for who they are. He doesn't judge or try to change anyone, but loves them for who they are at that moment. I will miss daily workouts with Luke, deep conversations on the back deck, and laughs that make us cry.

I love Will Harahan. For reference, Will is a six foot four, 270 lb man with a goatee. For a moment, Will had aspirations to work as a bouncer at a nightclub, and if you saw him, you would not argue with his decision. However, once you get to know Will, you will learn that he is a gentle giant. Will and I recently got close during my senior year. We lived together, ate together, worked out together, and even went on spring break together to Jamaica on a mission trip. When I think of Will, I think of generosity. Will would do anything for his friends. He would do anything for someone he just met. When someone needs a ride, Will answers the call. If someone needs help, Will is there. Will is going to grad school for occupational therapy and it is very fitting considering his love for taking care of people. Will's dad passed away in high school and I have appreciated the conversations we have shared around the kitchen table. Will competed in a powerlifting competition and he came in my room to ask if he could put the Getchell Brother's logo on the back of his singlet. He has become a close brother and I am thankful for that man.

I lived in a house with twelve guys: Zac Meyers, Haden Getchell, Will Harahan, Charlie Michals, Parker Bos, Zac Elmore, Aidan Jones, Luke

Shoemaker, Tyler Hicks, Joe Cornell, and Ryan Murphy. We live in a hole in the wall duplex, but we have a lot of fun. I am grateful for all of these men. We are part of the Arcadian Fraternity. There are too many guys to name, but I am grateful for the Arcadian Fraternity. When devastation struck my family, a sea of blue blazers surrounded my family and comforted us. My sophomore year, a different group of seniors, including some Arkies, lived in the same house I lived in my senior year. Jack Elwell, Ben Meyers, Zac Murphy, Drew Schmitz, Chris Stamatopoulos, Kayla Beckley, Danielle Reiber, Becky Biernacki, and Katie Newcomer. I look up to these close friends of mine and I appreciate our time together. We have a ritual now that every Labor Day we get together as a group to spend time together. They have given me great advice and I have amazing memories with each of them.

The next group of people significant to my life and who I am today are a squad of women unmatched to any other group. Emily Damstra, Kennedy Vick, Nicolle Malson, Elise Renberg. Their group has gone by different names throughout the years, but my introduction started sophomore year when I lived in Phelps Hall. That year, I played more monopoly in my life than I had ever played before, or since. For some reason, we became addicted to monopoly, playing for five to six hours every single night. We kept a book and each time we played the winner would get to sign their name. The group playing monopoly consisted of Emily and Kennedy, Keaton Koning and Drew Hoeksema. This group helped me survive the covid years while we were at Hope. Junior year, Emily and Kennedy moved in with Nicolle and Elise in a cottage called VB. This group of girls became known as the VB girls.

Things in my Pocket

The VB girls, along with some other guys and I, make up a friend group we call the Skunks. Don't ask me how our friend group name became the Skunks because frankly I don't know, and I don't particularly care for it but it is what it is. It would not be right to do a rolling credits section without including the VB girls and the Skunks. They have made my college experience truly amazing. My earliest memories as a group include late night, post party eating pizza rolls and watching *New Girl* at VB. We have gone to Florida together. Back in my Tik Tok days, my most viral video was a video of Drew proposing to Kennedy as a joke at a bar. The crowd cheered, the DJ played Ed Sheeran and we got free drinks out of it. I recorded it and uploaded it to Tik Tok and it amassed over ten million views. This group is the definition of spontaneous. We are always coming up with things to do. We have had different rituals like Monopoly night or Monday night Applebees or Wednesday night margaritas. We came up with any excuses to see each other. I will miss the convenience of a college campus and the ability to just pop over and hang.

Before college, my best friend was Trent Kinnas. From elementary school to middle school, our dynamic duo was referred to as "Trethan". We went to church camp together up north at Camp Barakel every summer. At church on Sunday and small groups on weeknights, I would look for Trent and hangout with him the whole time. Whether Trent knew it or not, his friendship grew my faith. He made church fun. He was someone I trusted and shared some of my favorite memories with.

Outside of my family, one of my first friends is Jeff Davlin. Jeff and I were born around the same time and our moms both worked at Portland High

School so they both went half time and worked the opposite half of the day so that one of them was there to take care of us. My earliest memories are from the house on VanBuren Lane, where Jeff and I would swing from a rope hung from a tree in the woods. We grew out of that season and started school in different school districts. A full circle moment for me was meeting Jeff for lunch recently where he told me he was going to seminary to be a Catholic priest. I am inspired by Jeff's faith and he is one of the types of friends that I don't see often but will be a lifelong friend.

Mama! Last but not least is my mama! Oh man, I could write a whole book for my mom, and she deserves it. Talk about inspiration. My ability to sit here and write, this gift of wordsmithing and love for reading and writing comes directly from my mom. My intelligence and my confidence comes from my mom. When I was little, she spent countless nights reading me books. As I got older, reading books transitioned to writing papers. She taught me how to write a paper. Not only as a mother, but as a teacher. I had my mom as my teacher for three out of four years in high school. Some people say they wouldn't like that, but I am such a mama's boy. And she didn't make class any easier for me. If anything, she made it harder. Thankfully, this helped me succeed in AP Literature and AP Language, and grew my passion for writing.

My mom taught me how to be confident. When I started having presentations to give, she made me stand up in front of her and give my speech to her. She encouraged me to speak slowly and not use filler words. She taught me to stand tall and walk straight. When kids were bullying me in school, she told me to punch them in the throat. I never punched anyone in the throat, and more realistically she taught me how to use my words. Use my words to express myself, and maybe cut back quick with something witty. This would usually keep the bullies at bay.

Intelligence, confidence, strength and love. My mom is so strong. And she has so much love. She made her job raising my brothers and I so that we would have a life that was better than hers. She set aside her own friendships and goals in order to help us build our own friendships and pursue our dreams. Growing up, she insisted that we invite our friends over to our house. She loves to be the host and provide a space for people to enjoy, let their hair down and be themselves. As cheesy as it sounds, I owe my accomplishments to my mom. She inspires me and continues to teach me about strength and love. She has experienced hardship that no one should have to experience. And yet, her perspective is to figure out a way to use her experiences to help others. That is nurture and that is love. My brothers and I were well loved growing up. My mom raised us well. She should have zero doubts in her abilities as a mother because there is not a single negative thing to say.

When we are hanging out as a family, my mom sometimes feels singled out as the only girl in the room. Admittedly, when we are together we like to bring up the shortcomings of her parenting (like when she left Haden at a gas station) but it is only to poke fun and laugh. We could do a better job of showing our appreciation for our mom. I could do a better job of showing my appreciation for people in general. That is why I am writing this chapter.

When I feel the pen in my pocket, I am reminded that I need to be grateful. I feel called to write a letter or a note to someone expressing my gratitude for them. I believe there is something special about a handwritten note versus a text or conversation. A handwritten letter because an artifact of appreciation that lasts forever. It is something that can be held, experienced, over and over again. From these stories and this chapter, I hope you are convicted when you see a pen. I hope you stop and write a letter to that person you have been meaning to thank. Or at the very least, I hope you think about it. It is valuable to have a posture of gratitude where you are constantly thinking about who and what you are thankful for. There is just not enough time for me to write it all here.

Things in my Pocket

Eight

Cross

I carry a little, wooden cross with me at all times. Sometimes people see it and I can use it as a chance to share my testimony. When I was in second grade, I accepted Jesus into my life. It felt right and it was intentional, but I did not fully understand what it meant. I grew up going to a non-denominational church that emphasized an emotional love for God fostered by a community of people who lived their faith out by being there for one another. The earliest memories of my life are filled by the people of South Church as my family spent time together in bible studies. These relationships grew into some of the closest friendships my family has. We went on trips together, we camped together, we shared life together.

I would say middle school was the peak of my "innocent faith" as I filled my time with church on Sunday, youth group on weeknights and mission trips in the summer. I say innocent faith because I had not been exposed to the harshness of the world yet. I lived a privileged life with two parents who loved each other, brothers that supported each other, and friends who cared for me. I had never been to a funeral and the most traumatic life experience up to that point was the death of my dog. I am grateful for this period of my life and I think it captures an important part of Christian faith that is the childlike innocence we are called to live into. However, this type of faith only extends so deep in maturity.

I did not learn this in high school, and frankly my faith was weakest during this time. I stopped going to youth groups on weeknights. I started playing high school sports which included wrestling tournaments on the weekends. This left me tired and I ended up not going to church on Sundays. My friends became the people I traveled with for sports events and the relationships centered in faith were put on the back burner. In high school, I didn't have a prayer life, I didn't read my bible, and what I experienced most evidently in high school was a lack of male fellowship and accountability.

Part of why I chose Hope College was for the faith aspect. I arrived on campus bright eyed and bushy tailed, ready for Jesus to fill my life with everything I needed. Second semester I met a girl that I started dating and thought I had it all figured out. She was further developed in her faith and inspired me to dive deeper. A month into our relationship, she broke up with me because "God told her to." I was sad to lose a relationship I cared about and I was angry that God would forsake me in this way. My weak faith was tested early, and it failed in this trial. After that I wanted nothing to do with God. How could a God that loved me hurt me in this way? I would wrestle with this question for the rest of the year.

In my second year of college, I once again found myself living a life of short term fulfillment with no regard to the life my faith called me to. I was in a bible study but I did not have a prayer life and more importantly, what I longed for yet was male fellowship and accountability. In the spring of my sophomore year, I was encouraged to participate in Exodus 90. This program is an extended version of lent where you practice giving up a series of sacrifices for 90 days. The program includes twenty minutes of prayer, seven hours of sleep, no snacking between meals, no desserts, no sweet drinks, no alcohol, no tv, movies, video games, no frivolous internet use, no social media, and cold showers. I had two accountability partners, Alec Kowalski and Jared Poliskey, and we had a large group meeting once a week with the advisor of the program, Father Nick Monco.

I am not Catholic and I did not know anything about the Catholic faith, even growing up in a predominantly Catholic community in my hometown. Catholicism to me was always something that people said they were but never explained what it meant. Before college, I had never met a Catholic priest and I had never done theological studying into what Catholicism, or even Protestant faith meant. This experience was the start to my development as a Christian. I did not have the goal to accomplish the program with 100% perfection. However, I was intentional about establishing a prayer life and creating my own relationship with God.

At the end of the 90 days, on May 2, 2021, I was baptized in Lake Michigan. This is a significant time stamp in my life and I chose Lake Michigan because at the time I did not have a church home. I had not been to South Church in years and I only periodically attended Pillar Church in

Holland at that point. However, I was born and raised in Michigan and my faith was planted and grown here, so it felt right to be baptized in its waters.

Paul Boersma is a close mentor of mine and retired Chaplain at Hope. I asked him to baptize me and he curated the whole event. My friends and family came. Everyone that was instrumental to my faith was there. We sang a few songs and I shared an excerpt from a letter my Granny wrote me that has been significant to my faith formation. Here is what she wrote me:

"Dearest Ethan -

Every parent rejoices in the upright choices and actions of children. And I believe the same is true of God. You are a Getchell, and that name means something, and you want to uphold its reputation among all people. The same is true of being a Christian. (And I'll confess that thought has a lot to do with why I've never put an ichthus on my car…)

Now here is something I encourage you to learn early. Just as a parent disciplines a child to keep him from doing something harmful, so it is with our heavenly Father. In other words, if we are truly one of His, He won't let us get away with anything that is harmful to us (and to our reputation, and thus to His name as well). We will be disciplined. Remember whose son you are - both physically and spiritually - and act in the manner you know both would approve - no matter what others around you are doing! You may not be popular with the guys and gals - but is that your main objective in life?

You know Romans 12:2? 2 Do not allow this world to mold you in its own image.

Instead, be transformed from the inside out by renewing your mind. As a result, you will be able to discern what God wills and whatever God finds good, pleasing, and complete.

If you check The Message paraphrase, you'll find it expressed this way: 1-2 So here's what I want you to do, God helping you: Take your everyday, ordinary life-your sleeping, eating, going-to-work, and walking-around life- and place it before God as an offering. Embracing what God does for you is the best thing you can do for Him. Don't become so well-adjusted to your culture that you fit into it without even thinking. Instead, fix your attention on God. You'll be changed from the inside out. Readily recognize what He wants from you, and quickly respond to it. Unlike the culture around you, always dragging you down to its level of immaturity, God brings the best out of you, develops well-formed maturity
in you.

In closing, I offer you an excerpt from a letter written by C.S. Lewis to a friend: No amount of falls will really undo us if we keep picking ourselves up each time. We shall of course be very muddy and tattered children by the time we reach home. But the bathrooms are all ready, the towels put out, & the clean clothes are in the airing cupboard. The only fatal thing is to lose. one's temper and give it up. It is when we notice the dirt that God is most present in us; it is the very sign of His presence.

Love and a hug!

Granny"

That day I proclaimed my faith as my own. I no longer believed in God because my parents did. I proclaimed that I was done calling myself a Christian without living out what that meant. My baptism was the end of one season and the beginning of the next. A season of exploration, a deep dive into the intellectual, the theological side of religion.

I spent the next year reading and reading. I read everything from C.S Lewis to the Catholic Catechism. I read about TULIP and Calvinism. I read *Signs of Life* and the sacraments of Catholic practice. One of the most significant books I read during this time was *Letters from a Skeptic* by Greg Boyd. This book is a collection of conversations between a baptist pastor and his atheist father. The pastor invites his father to ask any question he wants, and argue any stance he has, if the father allows his son to give a rebuttal. The question that resonated with me was "Does God cause suffering? Why would God allow suffering to occur in this world?" A valid question from a father who had lost his wife to a terminal illness. I was inspired as I read the response from a son who had lost his own mother. He says God does not cause suffering, or anything bad that happens, but the bad that happens is a result of our free will, our ability to choose evil and not have a relationship with God. This goes all the way back to Adam and Eve and the fall of man. Since that day, we have chosen sin over God repeatedly. Faith is an invitation, otherwise we would be puppets to a creator pulling the strings. I believe we have a choice, we have freewill, that allows us to choose God, or not. This choice has consequences that affect not only our own lives, but also the lives of those around us.

It was easy for me to read this word and agree with it. It is much harder for me to experience this in my own life and still agree with it. Time and time again, I have been affected by suffering. The difference between Ethan as a freshman and Ethan as a junior is that I stopped blaming God. I stopped running from him when bad things happened. Instead, I leaned on him. I leaned on prayer. I watched as the short term, earthly pleasures left me unfulfilled and deeper a hole than I was before. Only through prayer was I able to be lifted out of this pit. Not through my own strength, but through the strength of Jesus Christ.

As I reflect on the maturity of my faith, three lessons stand out as the most important contributors to my development. The first lesson must be viewed through the lens of healthy masculinity, or lack thereof. It is hard to ask a teenage/young adult male to point out his trauma. Many have not done that kind of reflection on their life, and many have not experienced what they would consider comparable to the dramatic connotation of "trauma." It is significantly easier to ask that same boy to identify the memory of the time they were first told to "be a man." As the oldest brother, I was taught early on to "be a man" by babysitting my brothers, mowing the lawn, being responsible, etc. Two quips my dad lives by are "don't sit while you work and don't watch someone else work" and "go to school, get good grades, go to college and move out. Most importantly, move out!" Early on, I was taught the importance of work ethic and independence. Without explicitly recognizing it, I was subconsciously associating these characteristics with masculinity. A man worked hard, a man was independent, a man wasn't emotional.

Things in my Pocket

Growing up in faith with these underlying expectations led to a life of navigating faith on my own without the help of others, without male fellowship, without accountability. Society told me to have it all together and I didn't know how to be vulnerable and emotional when I was ultimately drowning. It has only been in the last year that I have lived into the value of emotional vulnerability. I can't do it on my own. I can't do it without God. I can't do it without community. At a macro level, a lot of damage in this world has been caused by a lack of value in emotional vulnerability that has led to the suppression of pain and the unhealthy projection of this pain onto bystanding people. Ninety percent of murders and ninety eight percent of mass shootings are by middle age, white males. Domestic abuse is the leading cause of female death in the United States. These statistics are significant, yet as a society our emphasis is reactionary.

I firmly believe there is a place to recognize privilege. White males are the source of significant historical damage. Minority groups deserve allyship and advocacy. Yet, as an ally and advocate, I have still experienced the harmful side effects of what our society currently focuses on. I have been raised being told that I am privileged, so I have lived my life accordingly. I did not value therapy because I was "privileged" and didn't need the support that other groups need. I did not value dependency and vulnerability. I am "privileged" so I must have it all together. In a world that is reactionary to the suffering caused by the privileged, I believe we need more energy on a proactive approach to healthy masculinity. This is a critique I have of the church. We claim to love all groups, yet we fail to take care of our own congregation and raise men specifically as men who live into healthy masculinity.

The second lesson I have learned is that Christianity is a minority. I have had the privilege of being raised in predominantly Christian communities. From Portland to Holland, even those who do not identify as Christian live out Christian influenced lives as stores and restaurants close on Sundays and people share a similar "midwest nice." In these communities, we have the ability to live "lukewarm" faith because we can claim Christianity for our lives, and the majority of people know what that means. We can have a foot in each pool, claiming to be Christian and live however we please. However, outside of these communities, and in the majority of the world, this is not the case. There are entire communities that do not know anything about Christianity. There are communities that know Christianity and actively oppose the religion. This leads into my third and final point.

The world needs Christianity. When I say this I do not mean that the world needs theology shoved down their throats. What they need is to see an alternative way of living that is full of love and peace. We live in a world defined as the Information Age (also known as the Computer Age, Digital Age, or Silicon Age) with more technology integrated in our lives than ever before. This integration of technology has bled into every aspect of human life; from education, to health care, to how we interact with others. Even though we have this technology and integration, we experience more mental health issues than ever before. Depression and anxiety caused by a facade of connection that people claim based on the number of people that follow them on social media. We talk to people online that we have never met in person.

There is no space created for authenticity and vulnerability. I fail to see how these two themes are unrelated, and I believe the core of Christianity is a counter-cultural battle to what society wants you to believe are social norms.

Therefore, we need to recognize the damage Christianity has caused, including how it has taught men to be raised, and we need to shift the energy from continuing to react to suffering and proactively teach men, and women, how to advocate for themselves and others. As Christians, we cannot stand on a pedestal and condemn others for the way they live. Instead, we must show them an alternative lifestyle filled with love and peace. We must do our part to fight complacency and the status quo. In a conversation with one of my friends, he criticized Christianity as the source of suffering and prevention of innovation due to traditional priorities. I would argue that the significant social movements in this world have been inspired by religion, by people that care about other people more than themselves because of their convictions. Christianity does not confine you to a box. It frees you from the chains of expectations and asks you to consider that this life may not be about you, but about a Heavenly Creator who calls us to take care of his creation.

Nine

Pocket Knife

There are a lot of reasons why I keep a knife on me. I first started making it a routine in my life after some advice my Great Uncle Bill gave me. He said, "There are two things you should always keep in your pockets: a pencil and a knife. If you carry these two things on you, you will be prepared for anything." The same way I make my bed after I wake up to feel accomplished and ready for the day, I put a knife in my pocket to give me the mindset that I am prepared for the day to come.

Along with the advice from my Uncle, when I see the knife or feel it when my hands are in my pocket, it makes me think of the past. I got my first knife in elementary school. It was a small, three inch silver knife with a small groove that you stuck your nail into to get the blade to swipe out. I got this knife from my dad, although I cannot remember if he gave it to me or if I stole it out of his room when he wasn't looking. Either way, my parents supervised my brothers and I anytime we handled a blade. In my elementary years, my family lived in a two story, white house in Olivia Estates on Jennifer Lane. In the front yard was a big oak tree. My brothers and I would climb the tree, sit under the tree, and break branches off the tree. We would sit and whittle the bark off of the branches and sharpen them into a point with our knives. In the backyard we had a swingset, a trampoline, a strawberry patch, a sand pit and even more trees. This was the universe of a six, eight and ten year old boy.

My brothers and I would jump on the trampoline, swing on the swingset and play with our trucks in the sandpit. As the oldest brother, I was the gamemaster. I would get my brothers to do every idea I could think of. Once we found a bee nest in our swingset and I turned it into a mission to destroy it ourselves. We dressed up in last year's Halloween costumes so we wouldn't get stung and armed ourselves with water guns, fly swatters and bug spray. Superman, Zorro, and Captain Hook ran around the swingset, screaming as we tried to keep bees off us with our squirt guns.

After learning about cows in school and how they chew their cud, I went home and invented the game cows to play with my brothers. We simply crawled around the backyard on all fours, biting the grass and mooing at the top of our lungs. This game was quickly discouraged by our mom. I once helped my brothers steal the grill cover so we could use it as a parachute, jumping off our swingset to see who could float the longest. This game was also not approved by my mom. There are a lot of memories in that backyard. The oldest memories go back to when I was too small to remember. But through pictures and stories, I have come to learn about my early childhood.

I was *the* fattest baby you have ever seen. My mom has pictures of me dressed up for photo shoots in outfits like I was at the beach or the fourth of July. Regardless of my size, my mom had me, and then both my younger brothers, completely natural child births. I was born exactly on schedule, and have never been late to anything since… My parents settled down in Portland, Michigan so my mom could teach at the high school and my dad could commute to Lansing for work in thirty minutes. We lived on a farm that was right behind a golf course. We raised some cows and chickens, but my parents quickly learned they were not made to be farmers. The neighbor's dog ended up killing all the chickens and my parents couldn't keep up with the lifestyle of raising cows while also working nine to five jobs. There's an old video of me laughing hysterically at a cow with a bucket stuck on its head, running around freaked out and confused. I wasn't old enough to remember that part of my childhood but the people on Van Buren Lane are some of the most special people in my life to this day.

Two years after me, on August 30, 2003, Haden Thomas Getchell was born. Two and a half years from that, on February 28, 2006, Austin John Getchell was born. A brunette, a blonde and redhead. Looking back at old pictures of dad and his brothers growing up, they had a darker blonde, a lighter blonde and a strawberry blonde. I don't think my parents could have been happier with the outcome of their children. My mom always said she was born to raise boys. My dad wanted to name me John Wayne Cash Deere Getchell so you can kind of see where he stands in the matter.

However, I think a daughter would have been good for them. My mom would have had more of the communication she craves when the rest of us sit in the living room and communicate through grunts. "Uhh" translates to turn on the TV, turn up the volume, turn down the volume and stop doing that. What else do you need to say? My mom sometimes feels ganged up on being the only female, so another girl would have given her the defense she needs against us primal boys.

A daughter would have been good for my dad too because it would have forced him to soften up quicker. Teaching us to swim looked like him throwing us in the pool and waiting for us to bob up to the top and start laughing. He probably would have done the same with a daughter, but I think he would have become the stereotypical protective papa bear every daughter needs.

Life was simple for the first five years. My dad worked a lot and sometimes had to travel for work. My mom worked half time so she could get us ready for school and be home when we were. When my mom wasn't taking care of us, we were either babysat by Kenzie or taken to Miss Penny's house. Kenzie was fun because I would give her a hard time in the mornings. I would lie there, dead still, convincing her I was still asleep. I could keep control even when she would talk to me or turn on the lights. It wasn't until she tickled me that I broke cover - cheater.

Miss Penny's was great because there were always other kids there. We would eat all kinds of snacks and watch Spy Kids in 3D! That's right - she had the glasses. Whenever I rode in the truck with dad to Miss Penny's or to school, he played one of three CDs: Johnny Cash, Big and Rich or Go Fish. The perfect combination for any child. My parents put us on every recreational tee ball and soccer team there was, and coached us in all of them. There was also Awana, bible studies and church on Sunday. I remember sitting in bible school one Sunday morning with the rest of the kids my age, and the teacher asked us what we wanted to be when we grew up. I knew my answer right away and quickly raised my hand.

"Johnny Cash!"

I said with complete confidence. Imagine a five year old me in an all black suit with a cowboy hat. My ancestors would be so proud.

Life was simple for the first five years because after that my family experienced the hardest, life changing event we had ever been through. I don't remember what time of year it was exactly but I remember it was cold, as Michigan is most of the year. At this point, my family had already moved twice and were now living in a big white house in a small subdivision. I vaguely remember two year old Austin in the same high chair that Haden and I had previously used. He was sick with a fever. We weren't sure if it was because of the cold or because of the McDonald's playland we had visited.

It was after dinner and my parents weren't sure whether to let him try to sleep it off or take him in. Mom's Mother Bear instincts told her to take him in, and thank God they did because after running tests they discovered he had bacterial meningitis. Bacterial meningitis is a bacterial infection that attacks the membrane around your brain and spinal cord. It is the most severe form of meningitis and often leads to permanent disability or death. I was still not old enough to remember details but I vividly remember the pain. I remember dark hospital rooms, tears and prayers. Lots of prayers. I heard a saying that "a widow is someone who loses their spouse, an orphan is someone who loses their parents, but there is no name for someone who loses their child because there is no way to put words to that kind of pain."

Things in my Pocket

Things turned around for the better. Austin recovered but the bacterial meningitis took his hearing away - eighty percent in his right ear and twenty percent in his left. I remember little redheaded Austin pulling around an IV stand in his hospital gown while playing with Thomas the Train toys in the lobby, happy and clueless. The outcome was really a blessing because Austin had already started learning to speak and could still hear without hearing aids if he focused. Growing up, as annoying older brothers are, Haden and I would give Austin a hard time, sometimes more than we should. We invented a game around the dinner table where Haden and I would subtly try to say Austin's name between bites of food at higher and higher decibels until Austin would finally catch one of us. He would look up thinking his name was said but go back to eating thinking it was just in his head.

My brothers and I gave each other a hard time but we all love each other. Each of us have permanent scars from times we would rough house. Haden got banged up first with a scar on his forehead from when I was chasing him around the house until he tripped on a toy and hit his head on the corner of the fireplace. Mom was pregnant with Austin and the neighbors thought she was going into labor when the ambulance showed up. But no, it was just Haden bleeding out of his head.

Austin was the second one to bust open. Our family would go on bike rides pretty often and this particular time Austin forgot his bike helmet. We didn't think much of it and it wasn't a problem until we were crossing the bridge in town and my mom called Austin's name. He looked backwards and as soon as he looked forward again he ran right into one of the support beams, cracking his head open. This led to another ambulance ride. I was determined not to make the same mistakes as them and I was in the clear until one winter when we went sledding at the middle school.

Our middle school had a big hill that kids would come from all over to sled down. I had a snowboard that my feet just slipped into. I was walking back up the hill with my snowboard in my hand, looking down as I climbed the steep hill. I heard increasing yells and looked up to see Haden and Austin yelling at me to move out of the way. They hit me, clipped my feet out from under me and my head smacked the ice. I was more upset about the fact that I had to get stitches than that I was seriously hurt. The best part of that story is hours later, Mom called wondering where we all were and Dad answers with,

"Oh we're just in the emergency room. Ethan's getting stitches."

"What?! Why didn't you tell me?"

"Well, I didn't want you to get worried and stop cleaning the house." That is my family dynamic for you.

I grew up in Portland, MI where the population is around three thousand people. Everyone knows everyone. Everyone is like family there. People leave their doors unlocked and garage doors open and nothing is ever stolen. The town and the school are ninety five percent white, and that's being generous. To compensate for this lack of diversity, my parents hosted exchange students from all over the world. From early elementary school, my family has hosted exchange students every other year since I can remember. We had seven exchange students over about fourteen years. The students came from Thailand, two from China, Japan, Netherlands, Mexico, and Germany. We invited these students into our homes and treated them like our own family. On trips we would buy souvenirs, including pocket knives. The pocket knife that represents my early childhood became a representation of my culture. We shared meals and stories, learned new languages, and taught them how to whittle sticks.

I have had the opportunity to travel and visit three of them since I started college. My first trip was a high school graduation trip with my mom. In July, I turned eighteen and we traveled to Europe to spend ten days in five different countries. We flew into Madrid and spent two days in Barcelona. While in Barcelona, we toured the cathedrals and ate delicious paella. After that, we spent two days in Paris, visiting the Eiffel tour, the Louvre, taking a boat tour and eating cheese and wine. We tried to google a nightclub and accidentally ended up at a brothel, so lessons were learned along the way.

We ended that night at a bar called Gatsby's and this Frenchman asked if my mom and I were dating. I quickly said no and explained that this was my mom. He offered to buy us champagne. At the end of the night, before we left we went up to thank him for the drinks. He proceeded to dip my mom and kiss her. Great memories and funny to share that my mom was kissed by a Frenchman in Paris.

From Paris, we took a train to Amsterdam and met up with our exchange student from the Netherlands. We went out that night to different clubs, and late in the evening I started to get really hungry. The only place that was open was the European equivalent of McDonald's, known as FEBO. FEBO is a walk up Dutch diner with burgers that are showcased in little, glass doors. You take your card and swipe the burger you want and the window opens and you can take your burger. A genius idea that I took full advantage of. I ate more of those little burgers than I can remember. I also recall shouting that everyone in FEBOs was invited to my wedding. I love the Netherlands.

The last stop on our tour was Berlin. Our most recent exchange student, Florian, is from Germany. We stayed at his house and met his mom and his brother. We toured Berlin and ate amazing food. My mom decided to have a night in to talk with Florian's mom. Florian and I went out and met up with his friends.

We all went to the beach, which was on a lake and fenced in so they could close it at night. We swam in the lake and I taught the guys how to play American football. I don't think they fully grasped all the concepts and it just turned into "tackle the guy with the ball". It started to get late and they closed the beach so we had to leave. I was disappointed but as we started walking home, Florian and his friends started whispering. Next thing I knew, we were jumping the fence and going back to the beach.

At this point, it was dark outside, and I was wondering what big plans we had for sneaking back to the beach. However, there was no plan when we got back in and Florian and his friends just hung out in the dark. Apparently, they do this pretty often. When I think of the beach at night, I think of fires at the cottage. There was a small wooded area near where we were hanging out, so I told Florian and his gang that I would be right back. I dug a little hole in the sand, and started filling it with small brush. I collected bigger sticks and started a small fire with one of their lighters. They were amazed that I had started a fire, but I was just getting started.

While they were standing around the little flame that I only planned to use to light a bigger bonfire, I went back in the woods in search of bigger sticks. To my good fortune, I found a full size tree that was rotting and half broken. Florian said that his friends were all chatting when they heard this big thud! I came out of the woods dragging this log. There were concrete stairs that I dropped the log on to break it into pieces. I threw the pieces on the fire and next thing they knew we had a bonfire. There were a few public benches around that I pulled close to the fire. We spent the rest of the night talking about life around the fire. Florian told me that his friends call me the "American LumberJack".

Over spring break Haden's freshman year at Hope, he traveled to Germany and stayed with Florian. When he got back, he had a souvenir for me. It was a little pocket knife with an anchor on it. He thought of me because the anchor symbolizes Hope College. However, when I hold this new pocket knife, I think of my childhood, I think of my culture, and I think of the traveling I have done around the world.

I am grateful for all of the traveling and experience I have been able to have at such a young age. I am grateful for the people I have met, the cultures I have learned about, and the perspectives that are so different from mine. One of my exchange students is from Mexico and I had the opportunity to travel on my own for the first time and stay with him. Edi and his family are gracious hosts and we had an amazing time. They took me to see cenotes, which are these beautiful underground lakes in Mexico. We ate food like Cochinita, which is a traditional Yucatec Mayan slow-roasted pork dish that is prepared by cooking it in the ground. They even took me to see Chichen Itza, one of the seven wonders of the world. This history, this culture, this perspective has shown me just how big the world is and how many different ways of thinking there are.

The greatest lesson on perspective I have ever received was in Jamaica on a mission trip. We stayed in central Jamaica, the mountains of Mandeville at the Jamaican Deaf Village that is a part of the Caribbean Christian Center for the Deaf. Jamaican sign language is similar to American sign language, and we spent the week learning their language and communicating with the residents. During the day, we worked alongside them clearing brush, repairing fences and performing other tasks needed on the farm. In the afternoon, we went into Kingston, the city where the CCCD has a school and a coffee shop. The organization works to educate deaf Jamaicans and help them get into the workforce and ultimately to independence through community.

In Jamaica, they drive on the left side of the street. At the CCCD, they use sign language to communicate. These are all things that are different and "weird" from my perspective, but they are normal functions of life that the people of Jamaica have grown up with and do not know differently. They would think many of the social norms in the United States are weird. The lesson here is to understand perspective. No one is "weird", they simply have a different perspective on life. By learning different perspectives, we can gain a fuller understanding of life and what it means to be human.

Out of all the places I have traveled, one of my favorites is still Alaska. I love the outdoors and nature. I love the people and the culture. I love all the things to do. I have been to Alaska twice. Once fishing with my dad, and the other time on the May term through Hope. Both times, I brought a pocket knife with me for convenience and utility. I kept it in my pocket whenever we went on hikes. I used it to cut rope, open things, and repair equipment. Sometimes I would just hold it when my hands were in my pockets.

I started a tradition in Alaska for whenever I climb to the top of a mountain. With my knife, I carve an "A" into the rock once I reach the summit. Being on top of a mountain, I feel close to the loved ones I have lost. I am reminded that life is about the journey, not the destination. The pocket knife I carry is a representation of my history, my experiences, and my loved ones.

Ten

Coin

Hidden in the bottom of my pocket, covered by the other things in my pocket, and some lint, is a silver half dollar. I like to hold the coin in my pocket between my index finger and thumb when I walk down the sidewalk, feeling the face on one side and the United States crest on the other side. The same way this coin has two sides, it represents two opposite emotions. This coin represents memories of going to church on Sunday mornings at South Church in Lansing, Michigan. On Sunday mornings, I would walk into church with my parents and brothers. Every single week we would be greeted by Mr. Keys. Mr. Keys is an elderly man, permanently hunched over, with a thick Irish accent. Every Sunday morning when we saw Mr. Keys, we would give him a big hug. Mr. Keys was an important figure in my early years because he was a constant. He dressed the same, acted the same, even smelled the same whenever I saw him. After my mom taught me how to tie my shoes, Mr. Keys told me to loop the laces under twice when you cross the strings at the beginning for good luck. I double cross my shoes to this day.

Things in my Pocket

Mr. Keys never let us down with his consistency. His magic tricks that he would perform on my brothers and I are fond memories. After we ran up and gave him a big hug, he would pretend to pull a coin out of our ear. As a child, I marveled at this trick every time he performed it. As I get older, I reflect on his intentionality. I don't know how many coins Mr. Keys carried on him, but I did not only see him do this trick to my two brothers and I, but also to many other kids in my Sunday school class. This kind of consistent intentionality represents humility and care unlike any other. When I feel one side of the coin, I am reminded of Mr. Keys.

Just as there are two sides to a coin, there are two sides to the emotions and memories it carries. Although I am reminded of fond childhood memories when I feel the coin, I am also reminded of more painful recent memories. The coin I carry with me today was also given to me by Mr. Keys. It had been years since I had seen Mr. Keys because I started going to youth groups in middle school, stopped going to church consistently in high school, and moved away for college. It had honestly been about a decade since I had seen Mr. Keys, and even longer since he had performed that magic trick on me. During the spring of my junior year of college, when I saw Mr. Keys, it was not in church. He was in the visitation line waiting to hug me. What brought us back together after those years apart was the death of my youngest brother.

Through tears he came up to me and gave me the same hug he gave me years ago. He still dressed the same, smelled the same, and talked the same. But this time he acted much differently. The mood was much more somber as he approached me in the visitation line of the funeral home in my hometown. When he hugged me, the memories of going to church as a child flooded my mind. Joyful memories of time spent with my brothers. Overwhelmed, I crumbled into his embrace. At just the right time, I felt him reach up and touch my ear. Through tears I looked at his hand and saw the silver half dollar in the middle of his palm. I couldn't help but laugh as I took the coin and put it in my pocket. The rest of the visitation I held onto that coin whenever I became overwhelmed.

Whenever I hold the silver dollar in my pocket I am reminded of memories from the past and the emotions they evoke. I am reminded of my youngest brother, Austin Getchell. The first memory that comes to mind when I think of Austin dates back to my twentieth birthday on July 9, 2021. I was living in Traverse City due to a summer internship I was working at. My mom and brothers traveled up to Traverse City to take me out for lunch, and my dad would arrive later that day for dinner. We met at a restaurant just outside Traverse City and we sat outside on the patio under an umbrella that was protecting us from the bright, sunny day. It was a quaint restaurant surrounded by woods, as most of upper Michigan is. I remember my mom giving me the pair of airpods I had asked for that year, and I was grateful but less enthusiastic and more expectant than I should have been. I don't remember if Haden got me anything or not, but the most vivid part of this memory is Austin. He didn't have a present for me. I simply remember his big smile and rosy red cheeks, scheming as he said "Happy birthday!" and gave me a kiss on the cheek. I laughed it off as they explained how he knew he didn't get me anything so he told my mom and Haden he planned to just give me a big kiss.

I again was not as grateful for the act as I should have been, as it seemed like a lazy alternative to actually having anything to give.

However, now this is a permanent memory for me, emphasizing the love, the joy, the happiness that I shared with Austin. Part of why this memory stands out is because it is one of the happiest times I have seen Austin. Different things made him happy: his friends, his cat, his XBox, tennis, skiing, and his family. But in the last few years of his life, his disposition was melancholy and I think about that a lot now.

What did Austin teach me? What lessons did I learn from Austin? I always thought Austin was the smarter brother. I always thought he would end up being the biggest out of the Getchell brothers. Growing up, I would take Austin's side when he was in a fight with Haden. As his oldest brother, I saw myself as his protector. I wanted him to do well. I wanted him to do better than me. Looking back now, there were times when I would be sitting in the living room and felt like I should go into his room where he was playing video games and check on how he was doing. Instead, I would sit there and keep doing whatever I was doing. We "let him do his thing". Over time, I became more critical of his habits, challenging him to workout more, eat better, play video games less. My relationship with him digressed because I betrayed what I felt called to do. I felt called to check on my brother and I justified not checking on him for letting him do what he does. I became lazy and I neglected the comforting side of our relationship. It became a relationship consumed by constant challenging and little comforting. That's not how I was raised and that's now how someone is supported.

The biggest lesson I learned from my time with Austin is to be present and be involved. Go to the tennis tournament you don't want to go to. Have that hard conversation you don't want to have. Do not neglect comfort for the sake of challenge. This is brotherhood. This is mentorship. This is life and healthy practice for any relationship. Austin accepted people. He accepted his friends and his family. Austin accepted me more than I accepted him. Austin was a weird kid. He would tell you that. Austin also had a hearing impairment. Most of his life he had hearing aids and when he was old enough he had surgery to have a cochlear implant for his right ear. Austin never used his hearing loss as an excuse. He loved to read and he loved sports. In high school he joined the trap team, and even had an advantage because he could simply turn off his hearing aids instead of wearing ear protection.

My last memory with Austin was on his sixteenth birthday on February 28, 2022. His birthday was on a Tuesday night so the celebration was the weekend before or after. My family still wanted to celebrate his birthday so they made a reservation at Olivera's in Portland for that evening. I was in Holland, Michigan going to college at Hope and I had a class that met weekly on Tuesday nights. I asked my professor what he thought about me skipping class to go home for my brother's birthday, already expecting what he would say. He said as my professor he encouraged me to be in class but ultimately understood either way. Without his direct blessing, I went back and forth but decided to go home. Knowing I didn't have a gift to give Austin, I remembered his gift for me seven months before and laughed thinking about returning the same gift to him. We celebrated his birthday with dinner and it was so good to be together. When I got ready to leave, I got up, walked over to

Austin and said "Happy birthday!" as I planted a kiss on his cheek. I think he verbalized an "Oh man!" as he wiped it off in embarrassment while the rest of us laughed.

After his birthday, I went back to school and in March we had spring break. I went to Jamaica on a mission trip through Hope College. It was a beautiful experience and when I got home I reflected about it in my journal on March 26, 2022.

Saturday Night - 10:52 pm - Airplane to GR from Miami.

"Dear Lord, thank you for this week. Thank you for the memories and the experiences I was able to share. Your grace pours over me and my cup is full. I have not felt this kind of peace and joy and love in some time."

As poetic and metaphorical as it sounds, life can change like the flip of a page.

Tuesday Morning - 11:10 am - New room in a new house.

"My cup is empty. My heart is heavy. There is nowhere to turn to find comfort. Nowhere to turn to escape reality. Anger, sadness, confusion, grief - it doesn't feel real."

That Monday, I was having an off day. It could have been fatigue from a weekend of traveling home from Jamaica. It could have been stress from homework and responsibilities for the rest of the semester. It could have been a deeper spiritual disturbance due to what was to occur that day. I was going through my regular Monday schedule, which included boxing practice at the Sakwando Gym just off campus. I normally drive myself there, but decided to carpool with my housemate who had recently joined the gym; a testament to the off day I was having. I am usually on fire during practice, and I never get on my phone. That day I was extra tired so I sat down and I glanced at my phone; another testament to the off day I was having. I had numerous missed calls from my brother, which if you know him, is not unlike him. I called him back and I heard a distraught voice crackle through the line, "Ethan, Austin killed himself. You need to come home." I didn't respond right away, and I don't really know what I said but I hung up the phone and just stared at the ground. My first thoughts were "this isn't real. Austin is alive. Austin is at home." Then it was "Maybe this is a mistake. Maybe they got it wrong and he is just injured." Then it set in that my brother might be dead. I couldn't stand up so I squatted on the ground and started dry heaving. I went to the bathroom and tried to splash water on my face, where I noticed how much my hands were shaking. My coach asked me what was wrong and I just said, "My brother just committed suicide and I have to leave." I fell into my coach's arms and started crying. I am grateful for my friend Zac Meyers who drove me back to campus. I hadn't even unpacked from my trip to Jamaica so I just grabbed my bag, ran to my car, and took off for my house.

The car ride home was a blur. I remember sitting there in silence, half in reality as I kept the car between the lines but also half out of reality as my mind floated anywhere but what was actually real. I pulled into the neighborhood and saw police cars and an ambulance in my driveway. There were police outside and the superintendent of our school district standing in the driveway. Haden was also standing at the end of the driveway, wrapped up in a blanket. I got out of my car and walked up to my brother. I knew he had forced himself to be strong for my mom so that he could drive them home. I gave him a hug and said, "you don't have to be strong anymore." He broke down crying in my arms. The superintendent then told me that my dad was in the garage and my mom was inside. Reality still had not set in for me yet. I walked into the garage and found my dad on an old couch my brothers had collected to flip for a profit. He was on the phone with his siblings and I'm sure he had been making lots of calls to his mom and siblings to update them on the situation. When he saw me he hung up and we embraced in a hug. He kept repeating, "I'm so sorry. It's my fault." As a son who looks up to his dad, and who had never seen his dad in this kind of state with this kind of emotion, this memory is seared in my mind. I repeatedly told him it wasn't his fault. Reality still had not set in.

After I let go of my dad, I walked through our garage door and into the house. The first initial feeling was "home". I made this trec through the garage and into the house thousands of times, coming home from college to be with my family. The mud room looked and smelled the same. The same organizer on the right side was cluttered with shoes and coats and bags. The washer and dryer on the left made the house smell fresh whenever I walked in. I was hit with the same aroma and feeling of being home that I experienced with joy so many times in the past. This feeling was quickly tainted as screams from a mother who was going through the worst experience a mother can go through sliced through the air. I walked through the mudroom and turned left into what is our open floor plan with the kitchen, living room and dining room. I was overwhelmed and confused by the scene. Police, EMTs, and strangers I had never seen before navigated the house as they performed their responsibilities. In the eye of the hurricane, my mother sat in a wooden chair from our kitchen, just crying. This was when reality set in for me.

I broke down crying when I saw her. The dichotomy of emotions overwhelmed me as I wanted to hold my mother who was in so much pain while the other half of me, the little boy who was held by this woman when I scraped my knee or had a bad day growing up, just wanted to be held and comforted by her once again. I gave her a hug and we just cried. There were words of confusion, words trying to make sense of the situation, words of comfort that had the strength of a toothpick. There was nothing to do or say to make sense of the situation. A woman introduced herself as the caretaker, who explained why each person was here and what the process would look like. She brought us water and accommodated us however she could. Once I calmed down, I had so many questions.

Where? When? Why? Can I see him? Should I see him? Not being in a state to think logically, I trusted the advice from the caregiver, who told me not to go see Austin. I still think about that moment and I am grateful I am not scarred with that tainted image of my lifeless brother, but I so badly wanted to see him and hold him one more time. I then wanted to know the rest of the details.

Both my mom and brother had seen Austin that day. My mom saw him in class and in the hallways, cracking jokes and acting like his usual self. My brother saw him in the cafeteria and texted him to stop eating so much pizza. Older brothers love to give unsolicited advice. My dad worked from home that day, as my family was currently in the process of moving. It was not a hard move, in fact we were moving into the house across the street because it was bigger and is directly on the Grand River. Austin already had plans to make a fire pit on the river side and have his friends over to go fishing and make smores. My dad was getting boxes packed at the old house and unpacking boxes at the new house. When my family got home after school, Haden and my mom went to Grand Rapids to go shopping for a suit for Prom. Austin and my dad were working on moving and my dad could tell he was getting hangry so he left to go get some McDonald's just ten minutes in town. On the way he texted Austin if he wanted anything to eat and Austin didn't respond. He tried calling him and Austin still didn't respond. My dad still got him some food and returned home.

The new house is a few houses down from the old house, so my dad stopped at the old house to grab a few boxes before he went to the new house for a late lunch. My dad happened to walk into the basement and notice that the gun case was open. He didn't think much of this at first, as they were in the process of moving things out of the house anyway. But when he went to close it, he found Austin. A month after his birthday, on March 28, 2022, Austin took his life. Examples like Austin make mental health and suicide that much more complicated. There were no signs. There was no motive. There was no neglect or even, I dare say, any deep stress on his life.

They found a sticky note that he put on the door to the basement that must have fallen off. On it, all that it said was "Sorry for the inconvenience. Sorry for all the blood." When I read this, I read it with spite, with intent in his voice. Something made him angry. Maybe it was Haden's pokes to stop eating so much pizza. Maybe it was my dad's frustration with him not taking his shoes off when he walked in the house. Either way, he did not have an ability to process his emotions and weigh the consequences of his actions in that moment. I don't know what was going through Austin's mind that day, but when I think about it, I think about how he could have used a kiss that day. Or at least remembered the memory of me kissing him the night of his birthday. After I heard the story and had my questions answered, I went outside and stood on our back deck by myself. I was so sad for hours up to that point. When I was outside, all I felt was anger. I was angry that Austin would do this to our family. I was angry that he didn't communicate or think it through. I felt like his action was selfish.

That night after the ambulance took my brother's body away and the police finished their report and the superintendent left, my family congregated in the kitchen of our new house. In the silence, in the disbelief, in the pain, we went around and shared what we needed in that moment. Haden said he wanted to see his girlfriend at the time and maybe even go workout. Those were his outlets. My dad had already started making a list of people he needed to call and things he needed to do. That was his outlet. My mom needed her friends, her "tribe" she calls them, to be with her and support her in a way that the three guys in her life weren't capable of doing. That was her outlet. When they got to me, I had to think for a minute. I didn't have the comfort of my room or the spaces I loved in our old house. I didn't have strong connections in Portland of people I wanted to see or be with. After some time I said, "I just want to pray." My family and I held hands in the empty, new kitchen of the strange, new house and prayed together. We prayed for love and peace and whatever we needed that we did not even know to pray for.

I swear to you the minute we ended our prayer, there was a knock on our door. My mom answered the door and people just flooded in. Family members, friends, other community members that were friends of friends. My mom's tribe, my dad's uncle, my brother's football coach. The next week we were never alone. Our community came around us like I had never seen before. They finished moving all of our things from the old house to the new house in a day. They unpacked and furnished our house. They cooked and cleaned. When I couldn't think about anything, they brought me plates of food and reminded me to take care of myself. I am still overwhelmed by the love and support this community showed my family and me. In a recent conversation with a close friend we asked why these people acted the way they did. They responded that it was because of how we served them in the past. My mom taught their kids. My dad was generous with loaning our things to people who needed them. Years of giving without any expectation of things in return poured out tenfold in the week I spent at home.

From this experience, I have learned and am still learning today that there is an interwoven relationship between brokenness and beauty. In the wake of such loss, I experienced such love and support from my community. In the depression and anxiety, I build the tools to empathize with others. Lastly, I come back to the anger I felt towards my brother. I come back to beauty and brokenness. With the anger I felt, I learned to forgive. The most healing part of my journey was forgiving Austin. I wrote this to him:

Dear Austin,

Thank you for being my brother. I am thankful that our last memory together was your birthday. I am thankful that I vividly remember giving you a hug. I think it is beautiful that I felt that hug when I prayed for you. I know that you are holding me now. Thank you for letting me be your big brother. Thank you for letting me look after you. I am thankful that I have you to look after me now. When I am weak and tired, your memory gives me strength. We didn't have the same passions but we had the same love for each other. Thank you for supporting me in everything I did by coming and watching and cheering. I can still feel that support and I forever have you to cheer me on. I'm sorry for how I treated you. I'm sorry for the anger and the impatience and lack of support. I'm sorry for being angry at you. I don't know why you did what you did, but I forgive you. I find comfort in knowing you have found rest. You have been made perfect and now live in paradise. I would not take that away from you for my own selfishness. Thank you for your life, your brotherhood, and your love.

I love you,

Ethan

Things in my Pocket

Afterword

It has been a year since I lost my brother, and two years since I started writing this book. This book started as a conglomerate of stories I would write when I was alone in my apartment in Traverse City during the summer after my sophomore year. I started writing these stories because they were favorites of mine to share with others, like the story of how my parents met or how my roommate and I started a company flipping couches. However, there was no rhyme or rhythm to these stories, no theme or cohesion. I just wrote for the sake of writing.

A year later and I have life experiences I want to share with others. The pandemic, blackmail, and trauma. Yet, I still didn't have a way to combine these experiences and stories, and I had imposter syndrome feeling like I had no reason to be writing a book. But inspiration hit and I thought of *Things in my Pocket* as a reflection of who I am, the stories I have to share, and the experiences I have lived through with the spine of the things that I carry in my pockets and the answers I would have if someone asked me about any one of them.

Things in my Pocket

I am just a guy walking around things in my pockets. A person with a phone in his pocket that reminds him of the importance of human connection. A man with a wallet that represents his entrepreneurial spirit. A boy with car keys to a car that ties to his family. A student with a notebook filled with lifelong learning. A dude with a pair of sunglasses to go with his adventures. An athlete with airpods to hype him up. A grateful friend with a pen in his pocket. A Christian with a cross to remember. Someone who is always prepared with a pocket knife. A brother who holds a coin when he would rather be holding his brother.

Since losing my brother, I have battled depression and anxiety. Before 2022, I never experienced a panic attack. I never went to therapy or gave credibility to that line of work. After graduating Hope in May 2023 with a Bachelor's of Art in Business and Communication, I am headed to graduate school to earn my Master's in Social Work so that I can become a licensed counselor and pour into those who have been affected by suicide and mental health issues, the same way so many people have poured into me. I feel prepared and equipped with a toolbelt full of knowledge on how to handle these situations and empathize with those who are going through difficult times. I am excited for this next chapter and I carry the skills that I have learned from college with the newfound passion that is derived from the experiences I have lived through.

As a freshman, I thought I would follow in my dad's footsteps by majoring in engineering so that I could go into construction management. As a sophomore and junior, I planned to go into commercial real estate and even earned my real estate license. As a senior, I had an offer to work at one of the biggest commercial real estate brokerage firms in the world and yet as I sat with this opportunity presented to me, I was left feeling unfulfilled. Unfulfilled to a deeper calling. A calling to help others. Help those who are marginalized, without a voice, hurting and needing someone to talk to. I do not feel as though I am throwing anything away. Rather, I believe I am living what I am called to do in this world. Part of that calling is writing this book. I am just a kid who is going through life and wants to open up conversations that are not currently being had through my own vulnerability. Conversations on healthy masculinity, conversations on mental health, conversations on technology use. I am not specialized or trained in giving anyone the right advice, but I write this book so that others can walk through my life and allow me to walk through life with them. If not me, someone else. There are so many resources for anything you are going through. You are not alone. You are loved.

Made in the USA
Columbia, SC
26 October 2023